KAPTAN JUNE AND

'I shall never forget my first sight ᴏ...
magnificent, it stretched away in a flawless white arc ... serene, solitary
... I wanted to rush to it and embrace it like a lover...'

And the radiant morning in July 1995 when June Haimoff sailed into a
tiny, idyllic fishing village on a remote Turkish beach did indeed mark
the beginning of a new life, and of a passionate quest.

By 1984, Kaptan June, as she was affectionately called by the local
community, was living in a hut on that glorious beach. From here she
swam in the cool early mornings, ate delicious breakfasts of white
cheese and olives from the nearby mountains and watched the sun set
into the indigo sea. That is, until she met the sea turtles those huge
primeval creatures who lumbered out of the sea at night to lay their eggs
in hundreds on the beach.

Kaptan June and the Turtles is the story of the author's passionate struggle
– involving local, national and international authorities – not only to
save these marvellous creatures from the imminent invasion of the
entrepreneur's bulldozer but also to conserve the paradise in which they
lived from the ravages of tourism's concrete blocks.

June Haimoff fell in love that July morning and she was not going to
relinquish it easily. A solitary female in an Eastern culture, she tells her
story with courage, humour, compassion and, above all, hope for a
future in which all species may live together in harmony.

KAPTAN JUNE AND THE TURTLES

JUNE HAIMOFF

JANUS PUBLISHING COMPANY
London, England

First published in Great Britain 1997
by Janus Publishing Company
Edinburgh House, 19 Nassau Street,
London W1N 7RE

Copyright © June Haimoff 1997

British Library Cataloguing-in-Publication Data.
A catalogue record for this book is available from the British Library.

ISBN 1 85756 229 1

Cover design Harold King

Photosetting by Keyboard Services, Luton, Beds
Printed and bound in England by
Athenaeum Press Ltd
Gateshead, Tyne & Wear

Contents

Foreword

This is a true story of one person's fight to save a very special part of the world. A spit of golden sand, part of one of the most fabulous coastlines in the world, the Dalyan Delta, where people have lived for millenia, reaping a rich harvest from that betwixt and between world of land and sea. The ebb and flow of the turbulent tides of many centuries of recorded history, threats and hopes of every creed and kind have done their best and worst but the people of Dalyan lived on in that special sanctity of family life and a respect of nature, eschewed by the teachings of the Koran.

What more could anyone desire, to live with one's family in one of the most beautiful places upon this Earth, feeding on the organic produce of the fields and the freshest of fish from the sea, estuary and river, living in harmony with one of the wildlife spectacles of the world, the nesting place of the Great Sea Turtles.

This was the place discovered by June Haimoff only 20 years ago, 'dazzling, magnificent it stretched away in a flawless white arc, losing itself into the far distance under a summer haze. Serene, solitary and mysterious'.

Today, as roads, buildings, power lines, discos, traffic, earth movers, tour operators, buzz saws, supermarkets, ostrich farms, swimming pools, and urbanites encroach upon this paradise ... perhaps in a far corner of this planet, under a luminous sky where fair breezes blow, there is another sandspit. I like to think so and that there 'the voice of the turtle will be heard in the land'.

Please read this book and then like Kaptan June, Nergis Yazgan and all the other caring people recorded in this book, join the fight to save the living world upon which we all depend.

David Bellamy
Bedburn, October 1996

Chapter One

The Beach

I shall never forget my first sight of Dalyan beach: dazzling, magnificent, it stretched away in a flawless white arc, losing itself into the far distance under a summer haze. Serene, solitary and mysterious, it aroused in me a primeval chord. I wanted to rush to it and embrace it like a lover.

We were sailing in from the west on that radiant July morning in 1975, myself, Hansi and Reg on board my boat *Bouboulina*. We had come from Marmaris and intended to cruise for some weeks along the south Turkish coast. That morning we had looked at the Admiralty chart for the area and had noticed an amazing isthmus of sand. Now we were seeing it in reality, yet it looked unreal ... shimmering in the noonday heat, it seemed to be suspended above the sea and river which bordered it on either side.

The *Bouboulina*, a 45-foot converted Greek fishing boat, shaped like a pregnant banana, provided a comfortable floating home and each year, Hansi and I, companions of some years standing, took on a young man as crew. This year our man was Reg, a New Zealander who could shin up a mast faster than any squirrel; he also played a mean guitar. Hansi, a mountain man who earned his living as a ski teacher in winter in the jetset resort of Gstaad, Switzerland, had, in the space of a few years, become an excellent skipper. I, an English woman of indeterminate age and adventurous spirit, made up the third leg of an unorthodox trio. Our lifestyle on board was a carefree one spent exploring the islands and coasts of the Mediterranean and Aegean.

Now, as we approached that marvellous sandspit, a strong wind built up waves at the shallow entrance of the channel that connects the Dalyan river to the Mediterranean Sea. Indeed our nautical homework

1

had shown us that the channel was not deep enough for *Bouboulina* to pass through and now, as she leapt about like an exuberant porpoise in the agitated sea, Hansi turned her into the wind letting her sails flap and Reg ran forward to gather them in. Under motor we headed back through the rollers to the shelter of a rocky islet a few hundred yards offshore.

Soon our bow anchor careened its way down to the seabed and Reg launched the dinghy to take a line ashore and make fast to a rock on the island.

Leaning over from my place at the stern, I patted *Bouboulina*'s bulging hull. 'Well done, old girl,' I said ... for I regarded her as animate ...

Now I had a chance to observe the beach through binoculars and could see that the mysterious objects apparently floating above the sand were a series of platforms supported by stilts. Tilting at impossible angles upon these platforms were rickety shacks of various colours and sizes. Again, this mass (or mess) had the weird appearance of floating in midair.

'Let's have a look,' said Hansi, taking the binoculars.

'There are people there. Maybe someone lives in them.'

Reg had a look. 'I've never seen anything like that in Europe. Looks like Malaya or the Philippines.'

I surveyed the scene again through the glasses. Topsy-turvy, ramshackle, and endearing, some thirty shacks hovered absurdly in limbo. I fell in love with them on the spot.

A couple of flat-bottomed river boats now headed our way through the channel. We had read about these in our nautical 'bible' – Captain Denham's *Eastern Mediterranean*, and knew that they transferred yachtsmen who wished to do a tour of the Dalyan delta and visit the ancient city of Caunos.

Soon they were alongside and we were communicating as best we could. Our Turkish was nil, except for *merhaba* (hello) gleaned in Marmaris. Of the two boatmen only one had any English.

'Hello, yes, welcome, me guide Abidin Kurt, Dalyan river, Caunos, hot springs, welcome, me best.' The other man who had no English, nevertheless got our immediate attention by opening his mouth to reveal a set of metal teeth. Steel, silver, platinum, who could say, they were spectacular, flashing cruelly in the sunlight. But my eyes soon left his teeth and settled upon the golden-skinned charmer called ... could I have heard right? Aberdeen? Was there a Scottish ancestor somewhere? Slim, with sun-touched curls and gleaming *white* teeth, this apparition steered his dilapidated boat with impressive insouciance, by one sun-bronzed foot. Looking at this lord of the river and hearing his unique brand of English, there was no doubt in my mind as to which boat I'd choose for the river trip, but the boys were obviously riveted by Metal Teeth. Bargaining proceeded and finally some Marlboro cigarettes passed to Metal Teeth, and Aberdeen (could it be?) the Golden was entrusted with taking us on the Dalyan river trip.

His chug-chug boat was named *Diana* after the goddess of the chase, which seemed appropriate as his eyes chased mine in a flirtatious manner. Standing on the stern of his craft, foot on tiller, he guided us with aplomb through the channel's tricky passage into the tranquil river. As we coasted the beach I got a good view of the crazy encampment of huts on stilts and the people there. Some local boats were tied up to the shore. Swarthy men lounged in them or fished from the rickety landing stages; children played in the water and the three *restorans* bulged with humanity. We seemed to be the only foreigners in sight.

Abidin (I had established he had no Scots blood) turned his boat to the labyrinthine river where twelve-foot reeds lined the banks. As we headed north towards Dalyan a marvellous panorama was spread before us. Ahead lay a vast expanse of water and marshland bounded in the distance by a dramatic range of mountains. To west and east, cliffs and forest-clad mountains. At our backs, the flat, white expanse of the beach, silver sea and our islet silhouetted against it. A cloudless sky sealed the perfect beauty of the place.

As we went along, our golden guide maintained a monologue in his bizarre English, helped along by hand-signs and facial expressions of the ham-actor variety. At one point he laughed loudly as he said, 'Me mafia boss.'

Reg then tried out his one word of Turkish, *ekmek* (bread), which did nothing to check the monologue. Hansi made a surreptitious hand-sign to me – forefinger against temple meaning, 'this fellow is cuckoo'. I doubted it. Abidin seemed smart to me and I did not question his claim to be 'the best'. Subsequently, time was to prove me right. This jaunty fellow with the improbable name has in the intervening years become successful, known to yachties from all over the world and, though no longer slim and carefree, still knows how to charm. On that day in 1975 I made friends with someone who would one day, unwittingly, play a part in my future.

Snaking our way through the reeds, we gawked at the fabulous scenery. Soon, directly ahead of us, stood a dramatic outline of rock: 'The Lion Rock of Caunos,' yelled our guide in answer to my questioning wave. He had to yell.

Diana's engine had a roar that would have eclipsed fifty of that species. There was no doubt about it – the line of the rock was exactly that of a lion couchant . . . paws to the east, rump to the west. Settled on the small of its back one could just discern the outlines of a massive ruin and sweep of the theatre's tiers.

Soon our boat was tied up at the Caunos landing stage, another rickety affair, but this time with not another human in sight. Abidin led us past the fish traps of wood and wire where we could vaguely observe sizeable fish scudding around in the water. From our Denham 'bible' we knew that Dalyan means 'fishery' and that fish-farming has existed here since antiquity. Grey mullet are the principal catch, but eels also abound and somewhere lurking in the depths are to be found the delicious 'kings of the river' – the sea bream.

For fifteen minutes we now followed Abidin up a seemingly oven-baked path while he waved and expounded on the ancient surround-ings and the successive civilisations that had arrived, lived and died in this place. Fortunately we already had some notions gleaned from our aforementioned 'bible'. Up at the theatre, we looked down at what had once been an important, commercial port, famous for its export businesses of slaves and fish. It was hard to equate the silted-up little lake with a thriving commercial port, but historians have told us that the port was so important in its day that a chain was stretched across it and vessels approaching from the sea had to pay a toll in order to enter Caunos harbour.

It was also hard to believe that the magnificent delta did not exist 2,000 years ago, but was, in fact, the sea. And that wonderful sandspit too . . . so had the sea worked its way, taking away there, building up here, not only in Caunos/Dalyan but in many places along this coast.

Abidin made a fine picture as he stood on the highest tier of the Greek theatre pointing out Dalyan village and other interesting points whilst keeping up his semi-intelligible monologue. He spoke of the Caunos inhabitants of antiquity who, victims of the malarial mosquitoes, were known as the 'green people'. There were still mosquitoes in the area, though none around in daylight and these were later to present a problem to advancing tourism. But these were not our cares then and we made our way to the shell of the Roman bath to marvel at its size and the sophistication of its latter-day hot rooms, warm rooms and plumbing that worked.

Our next stop was Dalyan village for lunch. On the way we saw to our right the splendid Carian rock tombs, carved some 2,500 years before, resting places of kings and queens; their graceful pediments and columns seemed hardly touched by the elements while the empty eye sockets of their plundered interiors (centuries before) bore witness to the smooth hand of nature and the harsh one of man.

After lunch, eaten in a riverside café, we drank tea out of small glasses, then proceeded up the river in *Diana* to the hot springs where we soaked ourselves in the sulphur-smelling waters. This was followed by a cold dip in the Köyceğiz lake another couple of miles upriver.

Abidin told us more about himself and we described our lifestyles. We passed few boats, but he knew everyone of the *kaptan*s and what sounded like oaths were shouted from one boat to the other – *yok*s, *tok*s, *bak*s, *çok*s – these explosive sounds seemed to me to have an aggressive ring, but in fact it was all friendly enough. We did get to use our new word though, *merhaba* (hello), and aired it constantly from then on.

By the time we got back to the beach and its ramshackle huts it was late afternoon and we were ready to eat again. So we tied up in front of one of the *restoran*s – a grandiose name for this dilapidated shack which, tilting at an alarming angle, defied the law of gravity by not falling into the river. The sun's blaze against white sand hammered our eyes but, under the *restoran*'s straw awning with a strong south wind clamouring in from the sea, we were cool. In fact, there were no walls, simply rush mats some three feet high, a marvellous air-conditioning system.

A motley bunch of unshaven, wild-looking men shouted greetings to us as we sat down. We answered with our one-and-only *merhaba* to their great delight. A rich mixture of smells wafted around: grilling meat, woodsmoke, sweat, cigarettes. Cooks laboured and waiters rushed back and forth serving vast quantities of food to the Turkish families filling the twenty-odd tables. We were the only foreigners. The ladies, wearing voluminous bloomers with frocks over them, contrasted amazingly with the cooks and waiters who wore nothing but bathing trunks.

I took in this scene as though I had come home. Children ran around the tables and now and again one would be plonked on to a fat lap to be fed or petted. Some cats and dogs added their presence to the mêlée, skirmishing for fish heads dropped on to the floor.

5

In response to some staccato orders from Abidin, mountainous dishes of salad and fish stood before us on our rickety table.

As we tucked in, I thought about these tables, endemic to the Mediterranean or particularly the Eastern Med – one leg is always shorter than the others and one is for ever sticking a cigarette packet or other object under the spastic leg in order to prevent drinks spilling. As the Turkish scene washed over me and I sipped my raki, I pondered this phenomenon. Are these tables a speciality of Greek and Turkish carpenters? Is the short leg a sort of signature, rather as the great European cabinet makers signed their chef d'oeuvres?

Hansi had gone back to our boat to check the moorings. From the distance I watched him clamber on board from the river boat Abidin had commandeered to take him. He cared about *Bouboulina* and had been fretting all day. I was glad of his concern. It had saved us in more than one difficult situation.

Wailing Turkish music screeched near us on an ancient tape deck 'rescued' from some car or other. The exotic sights, smells, sounds and my first encounter with the powerful, aniseed-flavoured drink called raki gave me a sense of euphoria. Questions bombarded me and were interpreted by Abidin with the ubiquitous hand-signs and facial contortions. Where had we come from? How much had our boat cost? How old was I? Were the two young men my sons? I'd heard that before in other places. Our age gap seemed to bother a lot of people, so I dissimulated now – *arkadaş* (friends) using a newly acquired word. The Turks took it in their immeasurable stride. The quality of friendship, in those days, was nigh-on inviolable. So they laughed, raising their glasses of raki – *şerefe* (cheers), another word to be remembered and one I was sure we would be using a lot.

The sun was sliding down behind the western mountains. I knew we must be on our way, but could not bear to leave this happy-go-lucky atmosphere. These festive, untrammelled Turks and their extra-ordinary beach evoked qualities of childhood – a sort of belief that there *is* a Father Christmas or, in the present case, a genie of the lamp. An expectation of freedom and fun for ever more – an inalienable heritage. As we grow older, someone will try to knock those ideas out of us but here, I found myself in a carefree timewarp, unfettered, back in childhood again.

But we had other commitments then. We were sailors, involved with sea and discovery and *Bouboulina* was calling us to fresh adventures. So we left that gypsy-style place. Shouts, interpreted by Abidin as 'come back' followed us as we chugged off in his boat towards Hole Island. Wailing music joined the farewells as we headed through the now calm channel. Dogs barked, kids yelled, ladies waved fat hands and bearded men clicked their fingers as they danced the oryantal, giving us a splendid Turkish send-off. My fingers were clicking too. Reg stood up on the stern with Abidin, laughing as he tried to imitate the Turk's wiggling hip movements. Looking back at the huts sprouting out of the sand, I remembered my first adventure when I ran off to join the gypsies at the ripe age of four. That adventure did not last long for I was returned after a few hours to my demented mother. But I had lived free for those hours and mixed with children who lived in brightly painted caravans not boring houses. Those children did not have to go to school or to wash as often as I did. My flirtation with the unorthodox began then. Might I resume it in the future with these aquatic gypsies?

The glorious beach became a blur as we sailed off on *Bouboulina* towards the east, heading for new places, new experiences. Lit by the setting sun behind us, the sea changed from indigo to magenta tipped with gold.

Standing up on *Bouboulina*'s stern, tiller manipulated with one foot (à la Abidin), Hansi looked like a pagan youth. Shading his eyes with one hand he pointed back to the beach to the slapdash shanties shimmering in the distance.

'A place for love,' he said.

He might have read my thoughts. I went and put my arm around his shoulders, standing beside him, looking back. 'Yes,' I said, 'a place for love, a place to come back to.'

That was in the summer of 1975. We came back briefly many times, but it was eight years before I returned, then alone, and stayed in one of the huts. There I was to find a new purpose in my life and there to fall in love – not with a man, but with a place – a sandbar.

Chapter Two

Return to the Beach, 1983

In 1983 I came back to Dalyan beach after a chance meeting with Abidin Kurt in Marmaris.

I had sold my boat, the beloved *Bouloulina*, two years before as I could no longer afford the jetset lifestyle of winters in Gstaad and summers sailing around the Mediterranean. I had also separated from my companion/captain Hansi and life on board just wasn't the same harmonious argosy that it had been. For two summers I had attempted to sail *Bouboulina* with friends or paid captains, but no one matched up to my old skipper. There were the well-intentioned 'helpers' who almost put us on the rocks and the good-time Charlies who drank my booze and, when the duty-free ran out, left me to sail alone from Marmaris to Rhodes. Funk-scared I chatted up some Italians whose boat was moored next to mine and they gallantly and expertly brought us safely to Rhodes. I stayed there for some weeks trying to figure out how I could keep her, but there seemed to be no suitable solutions and finally, in September 1981, I did what I'd hoped I'd never have to do – sold *Bouboulina*. In fact, I was lucky to find a buyer at short notice and though the price was far less than I'd hoped for, I bit the bullet and, in a notary's office in Rhodes town, signed over my much-loved *Bouboulina* to her new owners – a young French couple.

The walk back to the harbour after the signing was one of the blackest times of my life and for the next few nights until I officially handed over the boat and flew back to Switzerland, I cried myself to sleep, desolate.

When I came back to Marmaris in the summer of 1983 perhaps the memory of Dalyan beach lay somewhere in my mind. I had spent much of the intervening time since selling *Bouboulina* looking for a place, a way of life, a retreat to replace her.

I heard my name called, 'Kaptan June' and there before me was Abidin Kurt − no longer slim as he had been some years before, but definitely golden and smiling as of yore. It was good to see him and to hear myself called *kaptan* as the Turks had done when I lived on *Bouboulina*. I clasped his outstretched hand.

'Where's *Bouboulina*?' he asked.

I told him. At some length, I'm afraid, so pleased was I to see this old friend of mine and *Bouboulina*'s. He was not alone but with a very attractive blonde who turned out to be from Australia. We sat in a café on the waterfront and over a few beers caught up on the events of the past two years, or rather I caught up, for I have to admit that obsessed as I was with myself ... I also told them of my recent divorce ... the parting from Hansi (whom Abidin knew, of course), the sale of my chalet in Gstaad and my on-going search for a sweetener to compensate for all the losses. In other words, I talked them almost into slumber ... when Abidin said, 'Why don't you come to Dalyan, to our beach. There's no place on earth like it. I've got two huts. I'll lend you one.'

At this point I have to say that his English had improved enormously, due to some years spent with the Australian, Jan, who now lived with him on the beach for part of each year. I'd abandoned my monologue for just long enough to learn that.

A hut on that memorable beach? My answer came with the speed of light.

'Yes. When do we leave?'

'Now,' said Abidin and called for the bill. We caught a minibus and travelled the not unattractive road to Dalyan, some 90 kilometres distant. I hardly remembered the village for I'd spent little time there. My thoughts were on the sandspit. At the quay we boarded one of Abidin's boats − he now had a *fleet* of six, and once more, with bare foot on tiller, he ferried us through the maze-like tributaries of the river with the high reeds on either side of us trying to make their whisper heard over the noise of his engine.

And so we approached the wonderful sandspit and my old friends the rickety huts, their stilts clinging to the sand, like burrs on a dog's back.

Abidin tossed the anchor nonchalantly and surely, and nosed the bow of the boat neatly on to the sandy shore. His two huts stood apart from the main clump down by the channel. We clambered ashore and crossed the hot sand, just a few metres. We were home. The two buildings, if you could so describe them, were masterpieces of unorthodoxy. Made of driftwood and remnants from ancient hulks, each had just one room and a large balcony, the structure supported by a motley collection of stilts, roughly hewn treetrunks. Some attempt had been made at painting the 'building' blue, but sun and salt air had toned it down to a delightful washed-out shade, something like a much-worn pair of jeans. Two wide steps that had once been red led up to the balcony of Abidin's hut, whereas 'my' hut was reached by means of an upside-down beer case placed on the sand. Doors and windows (shutters, for there was no glass) closed with the aid of bent nails and the only furniture in each room was a mattress. The roofs, covered with dried reeds from the river, re-affirmed the Robinson Crusoe character of the place. A strong wind from the sea caused the reeds to rustle. I stood in my room absorbing the sights, smells and sounds around me and surveyed the nails banged into the walls where my clothes would hang. It was perfection – the only jarring note being my Louis Vuitton luggage. It would have to go. A symbol of the past and of a way of life about to be ceded to the beach and the hut. I glared at it.

In fact, it did not all happen that easily, the change, the metamorphosis, but it started on that day when Abidin brought me back to the beach.

I stayed a week in the hut. Sometimes Jan and Abidin were around and we swam, chatted, ate together. Sometimes I was alone when they went off to Dalyan, or to Ekincik, where he kept his boats. Never once was I bored or afraid. There were some 30 other huts on the beach at that time, occupied by Turkish families, locals only, who came there to get away from the intense heat and the mosquitoes which plagued Dalyan. I could not speak their language but we waved hands and smiled at each other. Each morning I swam before breakfast in a sea which felt like silk and in the evenings floated on the still river watching the sun set beyond Hole Island.

The night before I was due to leave, Abidin spoke about the turtles. According to him they came to this beach each summer and laid their eggs. He had seen them.

'When can I see one?' I asked.

'They only come at night.'

That night we ate at one of the rickety restaurants and walking back I asked Abidin again about the turtles. He told me they nested near the sea not the river and so we walked slowly back along the wet sand near the sea's edge, peering and hoping, but saw nothing. I went to bed thinking of them and of their secret, solitary arrivals on this beach.

Next morning, before leaving, Abidin brought his friend Mehmet to meet me. Mehmet was to build me a hut for next year.

'1 haven't got time to do it,' said Abidin, 'but you can trust Mehmet. He's a good man. He'll build it for you.'

Mehmet spoke no English so Abidin interpreted in his usual histrionic manner. It sounded like they were having a fight but I liked the look of Mehmet, a grocer, who could also (apparently) built *baraka*s – for that was the name of a hut here. Later I was to learn that *baraka* is a word derived from Arabic which means happiness. After many *çok*s, *yok*s, *heb*s and other harsh-sounding words, Abidin picked up a stick from the beach and said, 'All right, where do you want the hut?'

I indicated an area of beach not far away, where a tamarisk and an oleander faced each other in more perfect placement than any landscape gardener could have effected. We walked over there and Abidin handed me the stick.

'Draw the hut. How big you want it. The rooms.' I scratched the outlines of my *baraka* in the sand. How simple. No architect, no planning permission, no land to buy, just a piece of sand to be rented at an absurdly low price from the local authorities, so Abidin had told me. And it would be in the name of Mehmet, for no foreigner, not even a Turk who was not a local, could reside on this beach.

But I was concerned about the price. Could I afford it, how would it be paid?

'Send him £300. The *baraka* will be ready in May,' said Abidin. 'You can trust him.'

I wanted my *baraka* more than anything on earth. 'All right,' I said.

So I left the beach in late September of 1983, looking back at that marvellous tongue of sand, marking 'my' tamarisk and 'my' oleander bush until they disappeared from view; my sadness at leaving tempered by the knowledge that I would have my own *baraka* in a few months.

11

Chapter Three

The Hut

In May 1984 I flew from Geneva, where I had spent most of the winter, to Istanbul and from there took an overnight bus to Ortaca, the nearest mainline point to Dalyan, a mere ten kilometres away. In those days, the airport of Dalaman had not been built. Now it gets as many jets per day in summer as Ortaca gets buses, for tourism has grown enormously here.

I lurched bleary-eyed from the bus in the early morning and engaged a taxi to take me to Dalyan. I was in a state of some excitement at the prospect of seeing the beach again and, I hoped, my hut, for telephone communications to Dalyan were extremely difficult in those days and Abidin had not answered my letters.

My taxi driver, who looked like a bandit, swarthy, wild-eyed and moustached, was obviously intrigued by the arrival of a lone woman and peppered me with questions as we careered along in his dilapidated vehicle. Raised eyebrows, cocked head and hands reaching up to Allah indicated to me that they were indeed questions. Of course, I couldn't answer. But that didn't bother him a jot, he continued on his way looking back at me not at the road, with his hands more in the air than on the wheel. Desperately, I sought a word to shut him up and turn his concentration to the road ahead.

'Abidin,' I said, then regretted it, for this produced head waggings, hand wavings and explosive sounding words until I recognised one – *arkadaş* (friend). '*Arkadaş*,' I echoed, as we narrowly missed a tractor teetering out of a side road.

Amazingly we got to Dalyan without injury and found Mehmet in the grocer's shop.

'You can trust him. He will build your hut,' Abidin had assured me and, indeed, I had sent £300 to Mehmet via a bank, or rather *the* bank in Dalyan, for then there was only one. But I had had no news in the intervening months and did not know what I might find.

Mehmet the Grocer greeted me with a handclasp and a big smile. I said, of course, the one-and-only-word remembered from the year before, '*Merhaba.*' The shop, a tiny affair crammed with shelves containing tins, boxes and jars with a baffling array of names and labels, gave off a delightful mixture of foreign smells – spices, herbs, pulses – these last together with rice, sugar and dried fruit, nestled in hessian sacks taking up most of the floor. A lurid calendar featuring a veiled lady looked down from one wall, whilst the great Turkish statesman and revered leader, Mustafa Kemal Ataturk, surveyed the room sternly from the other.

Mehmet reached above the top shelf and produced three hefty keys which had been hanging on a nail. He handed them to me, still smiling, '*Baraka,*' he said.

We sailed down the river on a beautiful May morning in Mehmet's fishing boat for, in the versatile manner of Turks, he was also a fisherman. Laden to the gunwales with nets, floats, fishing paraphernalia and my new luggage (Marks and Spencer), we ploughed through the satiny water towards the beach while swifts, swallows and tern swooped and planed over river and reeds.

How can I describe the excitement of waiting for the first glimpse of the beach? As to the hut ... the the sight of it, as we approached that great sweep of sand, left me breathless. Unvarnished, touchingly basic, it stood alone on its improbable stilts between the oleander bush and the feathery tamarisk tree.

My hideaway. Barefoot I rushed from the boat across the hot sand, up the three steps and, undoing the peg of the little gate, stepped on to the wide balcony. The scent of sawdust and resin was heavy on the air. The morning breeze whispered through the reeds on the roof. In every direction magnificent views of sea, river, mountains, cliffs, sandspit, all illuminated with the brilliance of the early Turkish summer.

There was no one about. My hut stood near the river, maybe a hundred yards from Abidin's huts and most of the other huts, which were in a cluster some half a mile away, beside the channel. In the distance I could see a few people moving about on the sand and guessed that these were locals or restaurant owners getting their places ready for summer.

Mehmet joined me on the balcony. With the hefty keys I unlocked the doors and explored my new home. There were two rooms of equal size and another half as big which would serve as kitchen/bathroom. Like Abidin's *baraka*, mine had no glass at the windows and the wooden shutters were held open or closed with a hook over a nail. The broad balcony ran the full length of the hut and was angled towards the southwest where row upon row of mountains disappeared into the summer haze. In the foreground, sand, sea and Hole Island and one could see from this angle how aptly named it was, for a hole about the size of a bus split the rock showing a patch of darker blue from the deeper sea beyond.

How I regretted my lack of Turkish. I wanted so desperately to thank Mehmet; to tell him how happy he had made me; to express my gratitude for the way he had kept his word and built the hut so beautifully and on time! All I could do was to grin my pleasure and make a few hand-signs. Later, Abidin would say it all for me.

News got around fast on the beach. I knew that from my stay the year before. So, I wasn't much surprised to see Abidin and Jan arrive from Ekincik in one of his boats a couple of hours later. There was, of course, no telephone on the beach or electricity or running water. Drinking water was brought from Dalyan in cans while washing water was pumped up by hand from beneath the sand. Toilets were another feature missing from the beach. That is to say – conventional ones – what they had were holes dug in the sand with wooden palings around them. When a hole became too unmentionable when passed on the windward side, the hole was simply filled in and the palings hammered into the sand around a fresh hole. Despite my passion for beach and hut, I was intent upon having a more hygienic system.

It was great to see Abidin and Jan again and we soon settled into a routine something like we had had the year before, except that I was now living in my own hut. They took me to Ortaca and helped me shop for furnishings for my place. Not that I bought much. I was determined to keep it simple. And so it was: mattresses on the floors; oil lamps; cheap cutlery and kitchenware; wooden spoons; low tables used normally in the villages for making *börek* (pastry stuffed with cheese or meat); striped cotton sheets and heavy boards for cutting and chopping. The only 'decoration' a naïve wall-hanging depicting four cats, dressed as humans, sitting around a table playing poker. That I could not resist!

Naturally everything had to be painted and/or creosoted. Gas cylinders brought for the two-burner stove; water tanks, pipes and finally wonder of wonders for the beach dwellers – a European-style toilet. With help from a Dalyan plumber who spoke a bit of German I

14

would have a flush toilet, activated by water pumped by hand from under the sand into a tank (an oil drum from a garage); another oil drum on the roof would be filled by bucket from the first tank. Mehmet built me a rough ladder with which I could climb up with my bucketfuls. It wasn't going to be easy but at least it was clean. Mehmet also put in an outlet pipe and another oil drum buried under the sand some distance away. A Heath Robinson sort of installation but it worked, but no one followed my example and one still had to take care to pass to leeward of the other lavs on the beach. Abidin already had a shower outside his hut and I had a similar one installed – behind the hut, on a wooden platform with rush matting to conceal my ablutions from passers by. The same tank on the roof provided water for it.

So the days flew. It got hotter, but the sea and river were near for cooling off. Until I got installed, Abidin and Jan offered me breakfast on their balcony – delicious affairs of Turkish tea served in small glasses, white cheese and olives from Çandir – the village where Abidin was born and which I could see nestled on the side of a mountain across the delta from my hut. Most days a passing fishing boat would bring us fresh bread and sometimes fish, which we would barbecue over a fire in the evening.

The nights were splendid, especially when the moon was up. At full moon the beach seemed more unreal than when I had first seen it, shimmering like a mirage under the sun's dazzle. Birds lived in my roof. And crickets soon installed themselves in crevices in the walls. I was not afraid, for Abidin and Jan were close and I had another neighbour quite near. He was a fisherman called Baki and soon we became friends as best we could without much verbal communication. I had bought a Turkish grammar/phrase book and a dictionary and tried to learn one or two words a day, but it wasn't easy.

Baki's hut, dilapidated and endearing, had achieved that marvellous, faded blue colour that I wanted mine to be. It would take time, wind, sun and winter storms to modify mine from the bright blue face it presented now, but time seemed to be an endless commodity on the beach. Standing on stilts as all the others did, his hut was almost in the river. A gardener as well as a fisherman, he had planted an 'avenue' of oleanders from the water to his door and as May gave way to full summer, these flowered a glorious pink. So did my bush in front of my *baraka*. Baki had a vegetable garden too where he grew melons and marrows. A wire fence bearing a grapevine enclosed it. This was necessary because cows quite often strolled the length of the sandspit, eating everything in their path, except the oleanders, which they are clever enough to know are poisonous. In time I collected a nice show of geraniums and other flowers in pots on my balcony, but had to be extremely vigilant about the cows. At their approach I would grab a broom and rush on to the balcony brandishing and yelling like a drunken matador. Baki and Mrs Baki did the same. She was a dear little lady who regularly invited me to drink tea on their balcony.

I walked the beach a great deal, picking up shells and driftwood which I used to decorate the *baraka*. One day there were some unusual spoors on the beach, treadlike marks the kind a tank would leave. Sea turtles! Suddenly I was sure they were made by one. Abidin was nowhere around. I grabbed my dictionary and rushed over to Baki's. '*Kaplumba*,' I shouted to the surprised man.'*Kaplumba*,' he repeated, looking mystified. I pointed across the beach to where I'd seen the tracks, then dragged him there. My Turkish was sufficient to understand what he said, 'Yes, turtles.' I was thrilled.

That night in the restaurant I spoke to Abidin about the tracks.

'Oh! yes, they come at night to lay their eggs,' he said.

'Only at night?'

'Yes.'

'Can I see one?'

'Maybe.'

'How big are they?' I wanted to know.

'Perhaps eighty kilos, nearly as big as this table.'

'Have you seen them?' I asked.

'Often,' he said, 'and the babies. The mother turtle makes a nest in the sand near the sea and the babies come out of the eggs a few weeks later. Also at night. Then they go to the sea. There are many of them, maybe one hundred or more eggs in a nest.'

I looked into the darkness that was the beach, for there was no moon that night, and thought of them out there, solitary and secret, maybe even at this minute . . . Surely I would see one nesting one night or the babies making their way to the sea?

The owner of the restaurant (or *restoran*, as it is in Turkish) came and sat with us. His name was Ömer and he had such remarkably long legs that I always thought of him as a stork. I was hardly surprised when Abidin informed me that Ömer was also a carpenter and a pilot, an air one not a water one . . . for I was getting accustomed to Turkey, the Land of Surprises, where lifestyles merge. When my plumber emerged from the hole-in-the-wall which masqueraded as a kitchen, bearing a large platter of freshly fried fish for our table, I didn't bat an eyelid. It was not beyond the realm of possibility that he carried a scalpel in his apron and could also perform brain surgery.

That night I lay on my mattress looking at the section of sky visible through the half-open shutter. A myriad stars peppered that small area and I thought of the infinite, of the beach out there, the delta, the beauty and my incredible luck at being here. Above my head,the reeds rustled slightly as the night breeze touched them. Fluttering near the window was a feather boa, a relic from my past ritzy lifestyle. And I felt a bonhomie towards all mankind, including my newly divorced husband. How could he have been expected to cope with someone who ran off with the gypsies when four and freaked out in a *baraka* when 60? For the first time he seemed to come into perspective.

All the losses, mistakes, traumas, angers seemed to melt away. Even *Bouboulina* wasn't as much missed. This sandbar was so like being on a boat – water on either side and all the sounds, sights, smells were there too.

Curled in a cosy cocoon I drifted off to sleep to the sound of waves reaching the seashore. The shore where the turtles came to nest.

And I seem to remember that just before drifting off I said, thank you.

Chapter Four

The Turtle

Next day early, after my morning swim in the calm sea (it was always calm in the mornings and rough in the afternoons), I walked further than usual and saw several turtle tracks. Some seemed to loop back into the sea, some were much bigger loops that also returned to the sea, and these larger loops had a disturbed area of sand at some point. I wondered whether that could be where a nest was? I decided that that night I would make a determined effort to see a turtle nesting . . . but I would do it alone. Somehow I had a feeling that it was something to be undertaken discreetly, something private.

On the way back to my *baraka* I spotted Abidin just coming from his shower, shaking himself like a dog. We waved. 'Come for breakfast,' he called. I went, but said nothing about the tracks or my intention to look for a turtle. That morning he had some fresh, dark bread called *pide*, baked on the beach by a lady who had an oven outside her hut. I'd seen some of the ladies working at their ovens under the sun and marvelled once more at the ingenuity they brought to beach life. Great meals were regularly cooked, especially at weekends when hordes of relatives came in their boats from Dalaman, Ortaca, Köyceğiz and even Muğla. No one had a fridge, except me (gas) and the *restorans*, also gas, and I wondered how they managed to keep things fresh, but they did. All supplies were brought by boat so provisioning was no easy task. I used to get things brought or would beg a ride on a fishing boat if Abidin was not going to Dalyan. I hated leaving the beach and seldom went to Dalyan.

A few tourists were to come to the beach that summer, brought by boat from Dalyan by one of the *kaptan*s and sometimes yachtsmen would come from Ekincik, on their way to or from Dalyan. At the big *bayram* holiday, which went on for some days in August, many Turks came and the beach at night was lit up with bonfires while drums and clarinets thumped and wailed. Sometimes I was invited to join the groups around the bonfires and so I learned the rudimentary movements of the oryantal and danced with them.

For once the day went slowly. The fixation of seeing a turtle was upon me and I longed for night to come.

In the early evening as I sat on my balcony sipping a drink and watching the sun setting, a visitor arrived. I did not know him and, at first sight, didn't care to for he looked pretty sleazy. I supposed he was a fisherman, for a tiny rowing boat laden with fishing gear was tied up on the shore in front of my *baraka*. 'Merhaba,' he said from the foot of the steps. 'Merhaba,' I answered. Should I invite him on to my deck? At that moment he produced a large and beautiful fish from behind his back and held it towards me. I invited him on the deck. He handed me the fish, which had a bright eye and had obviously been caught recently. 'Ahmet,' said my visitor, offering a rough hand. 'June,' I said offering my right hand, while keeping a grasp on the slippery fish with the other. The man behaved like a gentleman though he didn't look like one.

'Kaptan June,' he said and beamed. So did I. I liked this title bestowed upon me because of my sailing days. I offered my guest a cushion on the deck and brought him a beer. He produced a crumpled packet of the local cigarettes and pushed the packet towards me. I refused. So began my friendship with Insect Ahmet (Böce Ahmet) as I learned later he was known. To this day no one has been able to explain why he is called the Insect ... but I know now that it is common in the villages to qualify those who have the same names – so you will find Mehmet the Grocer and Paint Mehmet (the one who sells paint) and Taxi Ali, Concrete Ali and even Wine Ali (the one who drinks).

The Insect sat on the floor and drank his beer and only flicked his cigarette stub on to the sand when it was reduced to a few shreds of damp tobacco. He was squat, sturdy and darker than any Turk I had seen, in fact, he looked negroid with blue-black eyes and thick lips. I couldn't see his hair for he wore a baseball cap, so greasy and so formed to his head that it looked as though it had grown there, rather like a fungus. I was sure this cap never left his head, not even during sleep. But it was his feet that really hypnotised me. They were big and extraordinarily splayed in the manner of snow-shoes. Surely they had never known any shoes.

Conversation was slow to say the least, but I did ask him about the turtles for I was sure he'd know something, being a fisherman. My question elicited an impressive series of hand gestures, facial contortions and cries of *çok*, which I now knew meant 'many' or 'a lot' or 'very'. His hand indicated the sweep of the beach, his basalt eyes rolled up to the heavens, then he made pretence at shielding his gaze from the sun and followed it up with two hands waving back and forth against each other ... finis ... I took it to mean ... no sun ... nightfall.

I think Böce Ahmet would have sat there all night, but Abidin's boat appeared and he called to me to join him in the *restoran* for dinner. Ahmet and he exchanged a series of *çoks*, *yoks*, *teks*, etc., obviously they were friends.

Later I carried the fish to the *restoran* where they cooked it with plenty of garlic and herbs and Abidin and I saluted this king of the river (*levrek*) and Böce Ahmet who had caught it.

Abidin walked me back to my hut after dinner but this night I waited until he was safely inside his hut before setting off across the now cold sand to the sea.

It was eerie alone there on that vast expanse of beach but, looking back, I did not feel apprehensive for I could see a few dim lights from the huts, the familiar silhouette of my own hut and those near to mine.

I had gone about a half a mile along the shore when I spotted a dark shape ahead of me. A turtle? My heart skipped some beats. The object was lying half in, half out of the surf. I approached stealthily, hardly able to breathe from excitement. Was I about to see my first Logger-head? I crouched low and proceeded, somewhat like a commando, not wanting to alarm her. Then I saw I was mistaken – this was no turtle, but a large chunk of reeds broken from the river bank and washed up here. What a disappointment ... well what else but to go to bed? I started back towards the hut when, suddenly to the right, I saw it. How could I have missed it before? A dark hump about thirty feet in from the sea. I lay on my stomach and slithered towards it with bated breath, hoping that my presence wouldn't ruin everything.

She was half dug into the sand and was about the size of a coffee table. She was facing away from the sea and away from me – a good thing as she could not see me approaching. Slowly I crawled nearer until I could almost have touched her. It was pretty uncomfortable lying on my stomach on the cold sand. Her flippers made a slight rustle as she cleared the sand making her nest and she seemed to sigh, expelling air through her nostrils. Then there was a creaking sound as she shifted her weight. The hole she had made appeared to have a sort of tunnel astern and I soon knew what this was for, for there was a kind of 'plop' and an egg fell from her directly into the tunnel. It was followed by another and then another some coming in quick spurts, others after a pause. More sighs, heavings, shiftings and plop ... plop ... the eggs looked exactly like ping-pong balls. They were coated with a slimy liquid like egg white.

I watched, stunned and moved by this incredible scene I was privileged to witness, until, slower and slower the eggs came and at last there were no more. Altogether I had counted about a hundred. I was ready to cry, but not with sadness, rather with joy for this lonely, primeval creature come to repeat the life process just as her forebears had done through the millennia.

She rested a while then used her flippers to sweep sand over the nest, carefully camouflaging the area. Then she heaved herself upright and turned towards the sea. She looked even bigger when standing. I watched in awe as she lumbered to the water. At last I could stand for she had her back to me and so I followed her to the water's edge just in time to see the glint of water on her shell as she disappeared beneath the surf.

The encounter with the turtle was a watershed for me. From then on I began to identify with them and to seek knowledge about them. I wrote to various animal protection societies and eventually learned that 'my' turtles were the rare Logger-heads, or *Caretta caretta*, the second largest species of the existing seven worldwide turtle population. They are one of earth's oldest surviving species, said by scientists to have lived over a hundred million years ago. By comparison, homo sapiens is a newcomer with his fifteen million.

During the rest of the summer I read what I could about my new friends and I learned that they mature in 15 to 30 years; have a possible life expectancy of a 100 and an average weight when fully grown of 120 kilos. I learned that the eggs hatch in approximately 60 days and that hatching and nesting only occur at night and between the months of May and September. Their diet consists of small crustaceans, sea grasses and jellyfish. Logger-heads in fact perform a useful service by acting as marine vacuum cleaners, gobbling up the feared plagues of jellyfish which are the scourge of many bathing beaches.

On the beach I now regularly plotted the tracks of nesting females and their hatchlings. These latter were tiny tanklike spoors often to be seen on the sand in the early morning. To my horror I found one day a dried-up dead one. This, I learned, was the fate of any hatchling which failed to reach the sea before sun-up when it would dry out and die or

21

fall prey to seagulls or ghost crabs lying in wait for them. Local fishermen filled in my sketchy portrait of my new friends. In fact, they did not have much time for them and said, '*Pis kaplumba* (dirty turtles)', because turtles can damage fishing nets.

An intriguing tale came from Insect Ahmet who claimed to have known many a turtle. According to him, the males preceded the annual arrivals of the females by some days and lay in wait at a reef not far off the beach, like bridegrooms waiting at the altar. The mating then took place in the shallows off the beach or in the river near the beach. The Insect's explicit hand-signs and sounds made up for lack of verbal communication though, at that point, I could have wished for the help of a veil to hide my blushes and my mirth.

Other information, which reached me by mail via the village post office was precise and chilling – many countries of the Mediterranean were no longer visited by the *Caretta caretta*. Italy had reported but *one* nesting female and that in 1984. Greece's record was bad too – on the island of Zakynthos the turtle population was suffering because of destruction of nesting beaches on behalf of tourism. In an English newspaper brought to the beach by a friend, I read of conflict on the beautiful island of Zakynthos between developers and conservationists. Reading it, I trembled. Dalyan was so exceptionally beautiful, how could it remain 'undeveloped'? Would the present trickle of tourists turn into a flood? I'd heard rumours of a hotel to be built on our beach. How would that affect our turtles? Looking at the untouched expanse of sand and the few dilapidated huts it was hard to imagine it trodden by thousands of feet; peppered with sunbeds and parasols; neon-lit and pulsating to disco rhythms. Surely we were far removed from all that ... or was I guilty of wishful thinking?

Chapter Five

Storm clouds

The winter of 1984–85 seemed to drag interminably. Despite the fact that I was having a good time seeing friends and family and travelling, I was frequently uneasy and preoccupied with thoughts of my beloved sandspit and the turtles.

The rumours I had heard the year before about 'development' continued to worry me and as I read that tourism was rapidly becoming the world's biggest industry, I realised how vulnerable our beautiful beach was. So, in April when the weather was good enough to resume life in the hut, I returned to Dalyan.

My beach possessions had been stored for the winter in an old cottage adjoining Mehmet's house, this due to the fierce storms which occurred on the beach during winter and the presence of visiting fishermen who, seeking shelter for a night or two, thought nothing of breaking into one of the huts.

With Mehmet's boat piled high with my belongings, we negotiated the river, the words and tune of an old music hall song echoing in my mind – 'My old man says follow the van'. No cock-linnet to top it all, but my thoughts were wandering toward the idea of getting a dog. I had already been in that frame of mind the year before. The space of the beach seemed heaven-sent for a dog to run free. Why not?

Once installed in the hut, I began to look around at the familiar scene and to seek out old friends. The Insect appeared in his old wreck of a rowing boat and soon was doing his histrionic best describing a gale that had occurred in February and how he had been forced to abandon the sieve-like hut he lived in (he was the only person to spend the winter on the beach) for his equally sieve-like rowing boat. He managed to make it sound quite terrifying and I surveyed the peaceful sandspit with new respect, imagining the sea roaring across its width and making contact with the river. My hut was undamaged, but some of the more fragile ones were knocked about or had collapsed.

Abidin appeared the next day. His business was becoming so successful, he now had four boats and spent more time in Ekincik and less on the beach. Jan was in Australia and would come to Dalyan later in the year.

Abidin had got himself a speedboat and roared around in it, back and forth to Dalyan, Ekincik, beach, Çandir. His new craft struck me as alien in this natural setting and its high-pitched engine, which could be heard for miles on the waterways, was as offensive to me as its streamlined, plastic hull. I preferred the delicately shaped river boats with their flat awnings lying like wings at an angle, the whole creating a harmony with the surrounding reeds and mountains, though I had to admit that their chug-chug engines were gross on the ear. I visualised the glorious past when all the riverboats travelled under sail and oar; until 1940 there were no motor-driven boats plying the river.

It was too early for the turtles; they would begin to nest in May. But the kingfishers were there, iridescent blue and green, zooming off across the water at the approach of a boat or sitting patiently on a reed or post, long beaks pointed down at the water, ready to strike. I had words with the Insect about them. He had been describing his prowess as a hunter, eyes screwed up, finger on an imaginary trigger. 'What do you shoot?' I managed to ask.

'Duck,' he said. 'Moorhen.' Yes, I knew that many came to Dalyan in winter. 'And *balik kuş* (fish bird or kingfisher).'

I shuddered. 'What? Why?' I couldn't imagine anyone shooting these beautiful birds. The Insect laughed. 'For fun.'

My Turkish was improving and I now had to accept some ugly facets of local life, like shooting kingfishers. I had brought the Insect a carton of Marlboro cigarettes from England. 'No kingfishers,' I said, handing them to him, it might just work.'

The Old Man (my name for him) was on the beach. I had met him the year before and made friends with his wife and daughter. He spoke English and, though born locally, lived mostly in Istanbul.

Instinctively, I was not crazy about him. There was something sly in his glance which I did not like, but I was polite when he called, because I was fond of his wife and daughter. They had spent some weeks in their *barakea* the previous summer and we had drunk tea on their balcony or mine and talked at length. Rose, the young girl, spoke good English and was about to enter university to study English teaching. I took the opportunity to study Turkish with her and my own conversation improved greatly that summer. Mother was a serene, smiling lady who spoke no English. Now the Old Man told me that they would come to the sandspit in August. He had a boat and offered to lend it to me and to teach me how to negotiate the maze-like river. I was delighted and we began to make trips to Dalyan and to go fishing on the river. I was surprised when the Old Man refused to accept any money from me for the use of the boat; he only agreed that I could pay for the diesel fuel and bring him some Scotch and cigarettes when I went abroad. So, I learned to find my way on the river and no longer had to rely upon Abidin, who was increasingly taken up with tourism, and the fishermen whose timetable did not always fit in with mine, but I continued to wave 'hello' to them and to seek them out early morning and buy fresh fish, octopus and prawns from them. All was fresh and cheap and quite often they would rather receive a packet of foreign cigarettes than money.

When the Old Man refused to take money from me, I was impressed and thought my first thoughts of his being sly were a misjudgement. How wrong I was, I was only to find out with time. Other surprises, not always pleasant, lay in store for me, but in those early years I was starry-eyed and enjoyed the protection of the Big Man – Abidin.

The *restorans* were not yet open, but work was underway getting them ready for the National holiday (Islamic) *Şeker Bayram* (sugar *Bayram*). At night I would eat with Ömer, known to me privately as the Stork, because of his exceptionally long legs, in his ramshackle kitchen. Looking around me at the primitive equipment, I was again amazed at the resourcefulness of the Turks. Ömer knew a few words of English and I resurrected my meagre Turkish vocabulary of the year before. So we communicated over a delicious *levrek* or *kefal* (grey mullet) or *sigara börek* (cheese-filled pastry rolled in the manner of cigarettes); usually a heaped dish of salad and always large quantities of bread cut in thick slices. Raki, beer or wine accompanied these delights. Sometimes we were joined by a fisherman or two and occasionally the Old Man brought fish he had caught and we ate that; then I availed myself of the chance to learn about local things, for he could interpret. I asked about an unusually well-built hut which stood on a dune near the channel. I had noticed it many times on my walks and wondered what the letters ODTU painted on it meant.

'That's the university teams' hut,' said the Old Man, 'they are doing studies of the beach.'

'What for?' I asked.

'For building, I believe.'

'Building on the beach?' I felt panic-stricken ... on *my* beach...

'There are many rumours,' said the Old Man, puffing a cloud of smoke in my direction, for he was a chainsmoker. 'A yacht marina. A hotel at the other end of the beach. Another hotel across the channel from here. No one knows for sure. But they will be here before long; they come at least twice a year. You can talk to them, maybe they know what's going on.'

I was curious about the ODTU. The Old Man explained. 'In English it reads METU. Middle Eastern Technical University. It is an excellent one, in Ankara.'

From then on, when I passed the hut, I felt uneasy. Who were these people, measuring and messing about with my beach? What sinister intentions lay behind their visits to this lovely place? I awaited their arrival with impatience.

In the meantime, there was plenty to occupy me on the beach. I put the hut in order and got my 'garden' going again; this consisted of a number of old cans, painted various colours and containing plants hardy enough to thrive on the beach. Geraniums were the stars, flowering all season; cacti and palms flourished and, against all odds in this arid environment, a pampas grass in a bucket survived. In front of the *baraka* the oleander put forth new shoots and as May gave way to June, opened its tightly closed buds to a mass of pink flowers. Behind the hut, the feathery tamarisk tree flourished, whisking its branches to the sea breeze.

Each morning I swam before breakfast in the calm sea. Each day I walked the length of the beach four and a half kilometres to Iztuzu at the eastern end and then back the other way to its western end, by the channel. There were wonderful shells near the seashore. I collected some and began to decorate the walls of my tiny bathroom with them. Driftwood fascinated me and I used some beautiful pieces as decoration on the deck of the hut. I also found an ironic appeal in some of the other debris thrown up by the sea and began to create sculptures with wrecked shoes (why do so many one-legged people lose their shoes overboard?); ballpoint pens; plastic razors; cigarette butts; fruit juice packets; corks and beer bottle tops. Slowly I created a fleet of detritus vessels, from sampans to tugs.

And, of course, as I walked the beach I sought the first signs of a turtle's nesting. In the second week of May, one morning, I found three sets of tracks.

26

The sight of the heavy, tanklike tracks filled me with joy. The turtles were back. I looked out across the sea towards the reef, thinking of the Insect's story of the male turtles awaiting the arrival of the females and I imagined the female turtles, their eggs impregnated, waiting in the shallows for nightfall, for the anonymity of darkness, to come ashore and make their nests.

Not all my discoveries were as joyful though. One day, walking by the riverside I was astonished to find a group of tents pitched there. A couple of young men were sitting eating, tea glasses laid out on an upturned box, a pot of water bubbling on an open fire on the sand.

'*Merhaba*,' I said in greeting, then tried English for I was dying to know what they were doing there. Obviously they were Turkish and I had never before seen campers on the beach.

'We are surveyors,' one of the young men told me, 'we are camping here while we work on the other side of the channel. We will stay here about a week.'

Another young man motioned to me to sit down and offered me a glass of tea. By then, I felt I needed a brandy. Measuring ... for what? I remembered the Old Man's tale of a hotel to be built on the other side of the channel.

'What are you surveying for?' I inquired, dreading the answer.

'A hotel complex. Touristic, you know. It is a British company, together with Arabs. They will build a luxury hotel complex here.'

I sat on the sand and drank my tea, listening and chatting with them, hearing my worst fears translated into reality. They were nice enough young men and I could not bear them any grudge for the work they were doing. I invited them to come for a drink at my *baraka* when they were free and walked back along the shore under the usual peerless blue sky, as the sand-pipers chittered back and forth at my approach.

That evening I drank my habitual sundowner on the deck, watching the glorious performance of the sun setting over the layers of mountain ranges west of Hole Island and thought of my former jetset existence, marvelling that I was so serenely happy sitting here alone, uncoiffed, barefoot, casually clad, phoneless, carless, dateless ... and looking forward to more of the same tomorrow. It seemed I had found my lotus-eating niche, but I knew that that was only the beginning, the surface, the facile part – beyond lay much more. I was committed to the beach, the delta, the matchless natural beauty, to the turtles, to this, my adopted land. The conversation with the surveyors came into my mind. It was then that suddenly I felt vulnerable and afraid.

27

Chapter Six

One Turtle Saved

The second of the major Islamic holidays, *Kurban Bayram* (sacrificial *bayram* when the rams are slaughtered), took place in June and brought large numbers of Turks to the beach. The *restorans* bulging; drums and clarinets thumped and wailed; bonfires were lit at night and in the daytime families sat on the sand by the river shore of the beach feasting on copious picnics and barbecues. Children frolicked in the water while be-bloomered ladies chatted and watched them. I joined various bonfire parties at night on the sand and danced the oryantal, as they called it, wiggling my hips and clicking my fingers. All were vastly intrigued to see this foreign woman who knew how to dance like a Turk. It wasn't too difficult; I had studied dancing as a young girl and earned my living as a dancer for a few years. The holiday lasted three days and on the fourth, the beach was abandoned as though by an army in retreat, leaving a swathe of water-melon rinds by the water's edge and other less bio-degradable litter.

Soon after that I got something I had been hankering after for some time – a dog. I did not actually find Jo-Jo, he found me and it was love-at-first-sight over a plate of meatballs. I was having a snack one morning in a *restoran* on the river near Dalyan, called Gel-Gör (Come-see), when this cute puppy came up to my table and as good as asked to sample my meatballs. What could I do but toss him one? He dispatched it neatly. An enormous man lumbered out from the kitchen. I knew him. His name was Şeref (Honour), another of those marvellous Turkish names. Şeref must have weighed about 120 kilos; he was a fisherman, but again, in the inimitable fashion of these special people, doubled as a cook. Normally he piloted a large boat called, also, *Şeref*, though how he managed with his great girth to get on and off this vessel could only be believed if one had actually seen it. When not sailing his boat, he would lie on it in a provocative pose, on his side with one hand supporting his head, very much in the manner of Madame Recamier on her chaise-longue. Şeref was a superb dancer and I had had the privilege of sharing the floor with him, dancing more than one oryantal at various local weddings and such.

'This is my dog,' he told me in Turkish. Indeed I do not believe that even now he speaks any English.

'He is very beautiful,' I said, as the pup wolfed another of my meatballs.

'You can have him,' Şeref said. Just like that . . . but this was also very Turkish, spontaneous, unaffected.

'I'd love to,' I said, 'but what would I do with him in the winter?'

'He can come back here,' said the Fat Man. This was such a marvellous offer, I did not argue, but shortly after called for the bill, paid, hitched a lift on a passing boat and went home to the beach with my dog.

I cannot remember why I called him Jo-Jo. It certainly had no connection with anything Turkish, for the J does not exist in the written form in their alphabet. When spoken, the C sounds like our J, unless there is a squiggle underneath, when it makes a CH sound. A straight C written and pronounced in Turkish gave us Jo-Jo and my new little friend became my shadow and further enriched my already rich life.

Soon after that a cat joined us. Again it happened by chance and in a *restoran*, this time, in Dalyan. I was eating something when I noticed a weird-looking creature slinking under the next table; it looked like a cat, but something was not right. With a morsel of food I enticed it near enough to get a good look at it, then I saw what was wrong . . . it was in fact a young cat, not much more than a kitten, but it had been painted in blue and yellow stripes. I managed to pick it up. Its fur was stiff as a board. It was emaciated, in fact, possibly dying which made it docile enough to pick up. Most Dalyan cats fled at the approach of a hand or delivered a nasty scratch with their claws if the hand happened to be holding something edible. This cat was at the point of giving up. I held its pathetic frame on my lap.

'Who did this?' I called to the owner, a nice enough fellow who had recently opened this small outdoor eating place.

'The children,' he said and giggled.

I wanted to say 'It's not funny' but my Turkish wasn't good enough. An awful, mute frustration was upon me and I longed for August and

Rose's return so that I might continue my Turkish lessons. I returned to the beach with the poor kitten in my beach bag and she became one of the family. In the next weeks I carefully clipped her matted fur and cleaned off the worst of the paint with thinner.

The Old Man was playing up. I had no idea why, but no longer did he pay me his daily visits and when I wanted a lift to Dalyan he was never around. He had always been a busybody, scurrying back and forth between the *baraka*s, gossiping and catching up on news; now he redoubled his activities, except that he never visited me. I consulted my 'protector' Abidin, on one of those rare occasions that he appeared on the beach.

'I'll have a word with him,' he promised. I was glad, for I disliked this inexplicable behaviour of the Old Man and wanted to know why he was angry with me. A few days later, Abidin asked me to come to his office in Dalyan. When I got there the Old Man was already in situ. He did not look at me or greet me . . . something extremely unusual in this country. In Turkish he and Abidin then went at it in what sounded like hammer-and-tongs fashion. I sat still, listening, able to understand about one word in fifty. Finally, there was a lull and Abidin said to me, 'He says you owe him a lot of money for the use of his boat.'

'His boat?' I was stunned, for the Old Man had expressly told me he didn't want any money from me.

'Yes. It seems you've used the boat a lot and he wants something around half a million lira.' Abidin looked at the paper he had been scribbling on.

'But he said he didn't want payment,' I told him. 'I gave him cigarettes and whisky. Brought him a bilge pump from Rhodes when I went over there a few weeks ago. And paid him regularly for diesel.'

Abidin repeated this to the Old Man, adding quite a few stern-sounding *hep*s, *çok*s and *hem*s as I did some sums of my own.

'Here's my bill if he wants it that way. I think he'll find he has to pay me,' I said, handing my slip of paper to Abidin. He scanned it: four cartons of Marlboros; two Black and White whiskies; six pump impellors. Total: 850,000 lira.

When Abidin worked it out against the number of times I'd been on the OM's boat, he turned to the Old Man and roared in his lion-manner, 'You owe her more than you say she owes you. Get out of here or do you want to pay her?'

'Never,' yelled the Old Man. 'Child of a whore.' And he stormed out of the place.

'It's Turkey,' said Abidin. 'You'll get used to it, kaptan.' Would I? I wondered...

Abidin invited me to go and eat with him at Denizati *restoran*. Over a dish of succulent squid and shrimps he told me, 'You should get married. Life would be a lot easier for you with a man to protect you.'

Marriage. Turks seemed to be obsessed with the subject. Despite my greying hair, I had had several marriage proposals from total strangers since coming to this country. A taxi driver in Marmaris. A waiter in Antalya and various fishermen and lounging youths along the coast. All wanted to marry a foreign woman and go to her country: it was a firm belief that our streets were paved with gold.

'Just like that?' I said now to Abidin, 'without love or a common interest, merely to be protected... Oh! no, that's not my style at all.' In any case I wondered just how much I'd be protected, more likely domineered I fancied.

I told Abidin that I had a stalker on the beach... this chap had been following and pestering me all summer, but I merely laughed him off. I described his antics to Abidin.

'Keep away from him, he's no good.' I could have guessed that. Abidin speared a shrimp as though he was spearing the offending swain. 'Did he tell you he wants to go to England to learn English?' he asked.

'How did you know?' I said, startled.

'Ten million young Turks want to go abroad; this one also wants to get out of his military service and marrying a foreigner is one way of doing that.'

I had no intention of getting married anyway and told Abidin so. He appeared not to have heard me:

'I'll find you a husband,' he said. 'Just you wait.' I laughed. I was in no hurry to meet this Romeo...

Shortly after that, I noticed one day that the ODTU hut was inhabited. That same evening in Ömer's *restoran* I saw some people I had not seen before. A group of five men and one girl eating and chatting in Turkish. In answer to my inquiring look, Ömer came over.

'They are the university team,' he said. They looked pleasant enough to me and not as though they were about to destroy our beach. Ömer pointed me out to them and in a few minutes I was at their table and we had introduced ourselves. The leader, Professor Erdal, spoke faultless English. His companions were students in his faculty. Their studies of the beach had been going on for five years and were almost completed.

31

To a man, they all adored the beach and had no intention of destroying it, indeed, Professor Erdal turned out to be an ardent conservationist.

That night I went to sleep happier than usual. My fears about the university team's intentions were unfounded and what's more they were of the same mind about things as I was. I was invited to their hut next day for further discussions on how to save the beach and the turtles. Whoopee!

The new friendship with Professor Erdal and his young helpers embellished the intellectual side of my life on the beach. All were educated and aware and obviously delighted to exchange ideas with someone from abroad. When they left after a week, I missed them terribly, but they had assured me they would be back before the end of the summer and in the meantime, Professor Erdal had encouraged me to go on with my plans for protection of the Dalyan delta and so I set to work, composing a Proposal for the establishment of a National Park – Dalyan Delta. I had my typewriter in the hut and tapped away busily for the next few weeks, eventually producing a 12-page document of information and suggestions concerning the future of this unique delta. I had to go as far as Marmaris to find a photocopying machine, where I had several copies made. I sent one to the World Wildlife Fund; one to Greenpeace; and one to Brigitte Bardot. In the next weeks I eagerly awaited their replies, but I waited in vain. After a couple of months I did receive a reply from Greenpeace who told me that they had no plans to intervene in Turkey, but wished me well. From the others, I heard not a word. I had included many photos of the delta and maps, etc. I found it hard to believe that they didn't even grace me with a note of acknowledgement. It was a hard pill to swallow and did nothing to increase my self-confidence but I hadn't given up. I put my Proposal in a drawer and set about writing a letter of appeal to no less than the Turkish prime minister, Mr Turgut Özal. With copies of this appeal, I invited everyone I met that year on the beach to add their signature if they agreed with my desire to Save the Delta. Almost everyone I met did agree and by the end of the summer I had almost 200 signatures. One notable dissident was a German tourist, a man, who told me, 'Forget it, you're wasting your time, there's too much money involved, you have no hope. You cannot stop the development of this place.'

Rose and her mother came back in August and I resumed my Turkish lessons, sitting on their balcony in the mornings or late afternoons, for I and everyone else on the beach took a siesta in mid-afternoon. Both Rose and mother were keen swimmers which was most unusual among the women who came to the beach. Very few went in the water, even on the hottest days. When they did, they would go in fully clothed, bloomers, skirts and all and not swim but simply lie in the water. Rose wanted to wear a bikini or two-piece suit but her father had vetoed it. I told her of the troubles I had had with him. She knew nothing of it, indeed their relationship was a most casual one but she lived by his rules just the same and wore a one-piece suit.

'I know he is a dictator and I do not agree with him, but he is my father . . . he has made my mother unhappy for years and me too, but we must obey.'

I was quite shocked hearing this from Rose, an educated, modern young woman. In fact, Rose and her mother lived in Istanbul and the Old Man rarely went there, preferring to live in Dalyan, but they were nevertheless dominated by him.

With Rose's help my Turkish improved. Her English, already good, also improved through practice with me.

We spoke about many things sitting on cushions on the balcony, sometimes drinking tea, she knitting or crocheting, for Turkish women's hands are always busy at something or other. Rose was 21, dark-haired and handsome rather than pretty, a little full of figure and attractively feminine. True to the traditions of this country, she was a virgin and would remain so until her marriage. I asked her if she had a boyfriend, if she had ever been in love, would she marry, whom and when . . . the sort of questions women ask each other.

'I do not wish to marry and I have never had a romance,' she told me. 'My father made my mother too unhappy. I do not know if I will ever trust a man.' From what I knew of her father, I could sympathise with her but I said nothing. He was her father and I was certain she would obey him no matter what.

More tourists came to the beach that year. There was no sleeping accommodation for them but Ömer, a carpenter by trade, built a series of one-room what he called 'bungalows' next to his *restoran* and rented them out. They were basic huts, though each had a washbasin in it. The guests used the even more basic *restoran* 'toilet', or *tuvalet* in Turkish. I met all the tourists who came to the beach, for ours was a very restricted society. We would get together in the *restoran*s at night, Germans, English, Belgians, French, Irish. These were travellers, individuals or couples, not the package variety. All were united in loving the beach and its lifestyle. All signed my petition.

Turks came too, from Istanbul, Ankara, Izmir and many of these

33

were also interested in the protection of the beach. Conservation was a new subject in Turkey as indeed it had been in Europe 30 years before. As for the locals, they had no idea about the subject and when we talked about turtles, birds, flora, fauna and beauty, they watched *Dallas* or football on TV. Omer was the first person to bring TV to the beach and, in that year, 1985, *Dallas* had taken Turkey by storm. Most Turks did not have TV at home in those days, but watched it in cafés and *restorans*. The voices were dubbed into Turkish and I could not suppress a laugh when JR said to Sue Ellen, '*Nasil siniz JR?*' and he answered, '*Ben iyiim, Sue Ellen.*'

The local ladies were crazy about the series and believed that it faithfully depicted the life-pattern of all Americans.

One night when *Dallas* was not being shown, a cry went up from someone at another table – we were in a different *restoran* that night – Demir's (Iron's – another of those fascinating Turkish names). The cry was, '*Kaplumba!*'

I recognised it instantly as 'turtle'. A small man jumped up and rushed to the kitchen, then rushed back out of there wielding a knife. '*Kaplumba,*' he yelled and disappeared off across the sand towards the sea. I called to my companions to follow me and ran after the man. When we got down to the seashore, we saw a large *Caretta caretta* digging away in the sand, making her nest. The small man stood astride her, knife in hand, trying to pull her head up. I froze, then reacted and rushed at him confronting him across the turtle's back. I reached for the knife and, amazingly, he gave it to me.

'No.' I shouted in my best Turkish, 'No.' It wasn't very good but it stopped him. 'Come, let's go back to the *restoran* and drink a raki.' The magic word raki got his attention and he followed me docilely back to Demir's.

All hell broke loose when we got there – *Kaplumba*, they were all shouting, no doubt disappointed that we hadn't brought it back. I got the attention of the one who spoke the most English and asked him to explain to our friend, the man who wanted to kill the turtle, that it was a very bad thing to do. Why did he want to kill the turtle, I asked? I knew that Turks did not eat turtle meat. The small man said something I did not understand and then demonstrated with hand-signs. I understood, I thought and my interpreter friend confirmed it. We'd all had a couple of rakis by then.

'He wanted to make a cradle for his newly born son out of the shell.' I shuddered. A cradle. Then inspiration came . . .

'Doesn't he know there is a curse on turtle's blood?' I said. 'His baby would suffer something very bad.'

We drank another raki and parted the best of friends. I learned that the small man was a librarian in Ortaca – surprising behaviour for a scholar, but then perhaps he doubled as a butcher.

Chapter Seven

Friends of Dalyan

The beach was busy in late summer, busier than ever before. More *baraka*s had been built, more tourists came and even the turtles seemed to proliferate, for there were more tiny tracks on the sand as the young hatched out, usually a hundred or more to a nest. I dearly wanted to see a hatching but despite marking a couple of nests not far from my hut and getting up at dawn sometimes to patrol the cold sand, I never saw one. I did see a number of dead hatchlings, dried out by the sun, those who had failed to make their way to the sea before sun-up and I did find a few disoriented ones, still flippering madly in the wrong direction, and these I brought to the water's edge and watched them launch themselves into their element – these were satisfying moments to counteract the sad ones.

I had read that the hatchlings found their way to the sea by virtue of the glimmer which is always present, if faintly, on the water and that they could be disoriented by artificial light and head off in that direction. That summer some hatchlings were found dead underneath the *restorans* and I began to wonder whether the increase in activity on the sandspit, with more light as the *restorans* now had electricity from generators, whether these things caused the hatchlings to head for the artificial lights. I began to wonder also just how good our bonfires were for the Caretta Caretta. We beach folk were not late-nighters so probably the fires would not have affected the hatchlings but they could have deterred some nesting females. What to do? I felt helpless. I had no qualifications, no degree as a biologist, nothing tangible to give me clout to impose my ideas. I wasn't even Turkish. Did I have a right to try to change the status quo on this beach, where I was a foreigner? These thoughts would fill my head as I lay in bed at night hearing the reeds rustle on the roof and small waves breaking on the shore . . . In the end, I would drop off to sleep, comforting myself with the thought that I had an ally now in Professor Erdal and that he would be coming back in September.

Each day I would hear the distant 'crump' of explosions as they dynamited the way for the new road from Dalyan to the Iztuzu end of the beach. This dismayed me not a little for I thought of the birds and all the other creatures and the magnificent forest of pine trees and their destruction. For what? For tourism, of course, there could be no other reason. It was a strange situation I had got myself into here on the sandspit; on the one hand surrounded by beauty of a high order, on the other bedevilled by human behaviour which did not seem to respect this beauty. If only I could have forgotten all the negative things and simply enjoyed the sea, sun, fun, freedom, as though I were on holiday . . . but I couldn't.

Many friends visited me that year; the hut had a great success. No one wanted to leave, some even cried. The sandspit had an extraordinary effect upon people used to 'normal' life. They would arrive white-faced and tense from the cities and leave like bronzed gypsies. Music was part of our lifestyle too, there was always radio or a tape, playing everything from Pop to Prokofiev. Jo-Jo and the new kitten, Billie Holiday (so-named because she had cried the blues so loudly having the paint removed from her fur), played on the balcony or sand and followed me every morning down to the sea when I went for my pre-breakfast swim. It was an impressive sight to observe the two small creatures on that great expanse of beach, sitting by the water's edge for all the world like two lifeguards, watching to see that I wasn't carried off to Rhodes, 30 miles due south of our beach.

Rose also had a dog, a dear little white creature with long fur and a pointed muzzle. Rose doted on her and allowed her to come inside the hut, very unusual in Turkey. In due course, there was a mating between her and Jo-Jo. Rose was delighted and said she would give me a puppy. Even the Old Man didn't protest. I have to say that for him, he seemed to be fond of dogs. Unusual . . . as many Turks are afraid of them. This was useful to me on the beach, for, as a lone woman, albeit not a young one, I had my share of unwelcome male visitors. In fact, they became pests at times and I asked Abidin what I could do. 'Get married,' he said again.

One day I saw a posse of men arriving in an official-looking boat. They stepped ashore all wearing suits, ties and shoes, looking about as appropriate on the beach as performing seals. Then I recognised the mayor and the doctor. All morning they roamed around the sand – no easy task in the clothes they were wearing for it became fiendishly hot as noon approached. Then they fell into the Istanbul *restoran* (a new one built that year) and wallowed in a hefty lunch. I had noticed they seemed to be talking about the *barakas*; they even had a man with them measuring. I found out later what it was all about. Changes were to be made on the beach. The *barakas* had to be equipped with a toilet (indoor), some of then had to be moved away from the channel area and more concentrated together and they must all be painted *brown*. I was appalled. It sounded so regimented and unsuitable for this gorgeous, natural place . . . though if the toilets had flushes I could see that that was a good idea.

'Did they mention anything about the rubbish?' I asked. 'What rubbish?' he said. I should have known better than to ask. The one glaring problem of the beach which needed to be addressed was the one no one spoke of, named rubbish. People threw it out of their windows or at best buried it under the sand and some, like the Old Man and the *restorans*, took it on their boats and threw it into the reeds where it was eventually blown into the river. There were no litter bins at all on the beach and despite many complaints, we had to wait till 1987 to get some.

The visit of the bigwigs from Dalyan was the talk of the beach for days. No one wanted to put a toilet in their hut, it would cost money. No one wanted to move their hut. Painting them brown didn't bother anyone much, except me. I loved my blue, which was now beginning to acquire the desired faded-jeans look and, in fact, I never did change the colour and no one punished me. Strangely enough, the beach residents didn't seem to worry as to *why* these changes were to take place. I did. I was pretty sure it had to do with some kind of planned development, perhaps the building of the British/Arab hotel complex planned for the other side of the channel. The huts to be moved were all those nearest to the channel. Fortunately mine could stay were it was, some 500 yards down the beach.

Rose and her mother went back to Istanbul in early September. I missed them, but they had invited me to go and stay in their home in Istanbul during the winter. I had made other friendships on the beach and was often invited to people's decks for tea or food. One family had a charming, ramshackle hut with a vine growing across its balcony and a phalanx of beach lilies, white and scented growing in the sand in front of it. These were a delightful, hospitable family of mother, father and three children; the boy Yildirim (Lightning) was one of my absolute favourites. He would serve the dinner on their balcony – usually fish, for father worked for the Dalko Fish Co-operative. In the traditional fashion, father and I were served first. We sat at a table and had raki with our food. Mother and children sat apart without alcohol, for the majority of Turkish women do not drink.

After the meal we would dance, particularly Yildirim and I, while the others clapped and watched. We danced to Turkish music played on my cassette player which I would take along. Marvellous evenings and as I walked back home with my Jo-Jo, just a couple of hundred yards across the sand, sometimes under the moonlight, I would think how lucky I was and my preoccupations with conservation, human behaviour and the future of the beach would be forgotten.

Fortunately, my stalker was never at the beach at night or I would have been scared in my solitude. According to Ömer, who knew just about everything, the young man (whom I had privately nicknamed the Snake because of his basalt-type eyes and a speech impediment which made him sound at times as though he were hissing) lived with his mother in Dalyan and always went back there at night. By day, he fished or took tourists up and down the river on his boat. In between these activities he patrolled the riverside, passing by my hut, waving and smiling in my direction. I never waved or smiled back, indeed his interest in me was unwelcome. The only good thing I could say about him was that seen at close quarters he did have splendid, white teeth and that was a rarity in the region – most people had dreadful teeth – and those who had been to a dentist had replaced their original ones with gold . . . a disquieting sight, especially when glinting in the sunlight.

Once Jo-Jo came to live with me my stalker disappeared, for he was terrified of dogs.

Mehmet the grocer, who had built my hut, also had a hut on the sandspit and we would often exchange visits. His wife, Fatma, a shy beauty; his daughter Gülşa (Best of Roses) a pretty four-year-old and his two-year-old son, the chubby Mustafa. Except for myself and the *restoran* staff, no one stayed all the time on the beach, but came for a day or two, for weekends or national and religious holidays. Mehmet and Fatma treated me as family. On the rare occasions I needed to spend a night in Dalyan, there was always a bed for me in their house, preceded by a delicious meal cooked by Fatma. Slowly I began to be able to talk with them, thanks to Rose's teaching and my own efforts with a

39

Turkish grammar book and dictionary. I tried to memorise a few new words each day and would mumble them to myself as I walked along the seashore or motored up the river to Dalyan or back down to the hut. On Saturdays I joined all the local ladies at the Dalyan market, coming back laden with luscious fresh fruit, veges and bread, still warm from the baker's. No more did I travel with the Old Man, but hitched a lift on Ömer's boat or with a fisherman or tourist boat. On the return trips the boats were quite laden down, for drinking water had to be brought in cans, and gas cylinders for stoves, lamps and (rarely) refrigerators. Jo-Jo did not go with me but was always at our ramshackle jetty to meet me. Although all the boats had the same noisy engine, he could differentiate and knew which boat was 'mine'.

September had always been my favourite month – on the beach and, that year of 1985 it seemed to excel itself. Glorious day followed glorious day and the pyrotechnics of the sunsets were phenomenal. Also, they were shared, for I had many guests that month, who seemed to share my enthusiasm and lingered on. The cabins were full and at night even the ugly, new Istanbul *restoran* that had been built that year with the first *concrete* to be seen on Dalyan beach . . . even that had some guests in the evenings. The nights were a caress, still warm but without the discomfort of August heat and, of course, we also had no mosquitoes, while Dalyan residents swatted and lay awake at night cursing.

One day Böce Ahmet appeared at my gate with an impressive *levrek*, which he handed me. He then sat down at his customary spot on the deck, impossible splay-feet tucked under each haunch, baseball cap moulded on to head, ubiquitous cigarette stuck on lower lip. He brought a bad rumour with him. 'All the huts must go,' he said.

'How do you know this?' I asked.

'The cousin of my brother-in-law who works for Köyceğiz town council told me so.'

I knew that Köyceğiz played an important role in local decisions. It was the seat of government, answerable to Ankara and handed down orders to Dalyan and other lesser townships and villages.

I listened to the Insect for an hour or so, handing him a beer as required and understanding about a tenth of what he said. That night I slept badly. Was it true? Was our beach life doomed? I tossed and turned. Jo-Jo was unsettled too and passed most of the night on the deck or the sand, barking and seeing off imaginary prowlers . . . or were they imaginary?

40

At last Professor Erdal and his students came. It was almost the end of September when I saw signs of life at the brown hut, which now stood all alone on its hillock in the area cleared by the removal of the huts and *restorans* towards 'my' part of the beach. We enjoyed a marvellous reunion in their hut and talked for hours about the beach and its future. It was decided we must form a group to give us a voice and cohesion. 'Friends of Dalyan' was eventually arrived at. I liked it; it had a ring and would sound well in German, Turkish and English. We had seen that love of the delta and desire to protect it was not restricted to any one nationality. Our supporters would be multinational.

There was no problem about sleeping that night. I dropped off to the sweet sounds of the reeds on the roof, the wavelets on the beach and Billie Holiday purring, serene in the knowledge that both Dalyan and I had friends.

I was still on the beach in mid-October, although it was by now almost deserted. Only one *restoran* remained open, Ömer's; he was a beach-lover like me and hated to leave for another winter. Each evening Jo-Jo and I walked there and shared a meal with him in his kitchen. Afterwards he, or his helper Kazim would walk me back to my hut, a kindness I appreciated, especially on pitch black nights when there was no moon. By contrast, the days were brilliant and warm and I still swam every day and walked the length of the sandspit, looking out to sea and travelling in thought with the fledgeling turtles on their first journeys of survival or with their mothers swimming powerfully to warmer waters. How many of them would come back to this great arc of sand?

A mighty gale from the west hit the beach as I was packing to leave and I spent a terrifying night battened down in the hut as the wind screamed around it and the roar of the surf rose until I feared the water was at my gate. Cowering in bed with Jo-Jo trembling beside me, I thought of the Insect's account of the great storm of the winter before when the sea had crossed the sandbar. It seemed impossible that the hut could withstand much more of this battering from the wind and my thoughts turned to crazy plans of escape, but how, where ... up on to the roof was the recurrent, ridiculous idea, until, worn out with thinking, I fell asleep.

I awoke to a perfectly still morning with the usual sunshine prisming through chinks in the walls and the familiar twittering of birds. Opening the door I expected to find devastation and the sea within inches of the hut, but no, all looked the same as before, the sea in its old place and the sandspit serene; the only slight modification being that all looked newly washed as though with detergent.

Mehmet's boat soon turned up.

'Come on, Kaptan, it's time to leave,' he said. And so we did, possessions piled on board as usual.

From the river I looked back on the beach I so loved, but now I looked with new eyes. Nature had shown me her violent side, had made me afraid and I recognised my limitations as a beach-dweller.

Chapter Eight

A Diversion

So much happened in 1986 that it is hard to know the order of priorities, but let me start with my arrival back at the sandbar in April of that year.

Sadness awaited me with the news that my dear dog, Jo-Jo had been killed in an accident some weeks before. I cried. How empty life would seem without my little companion. Good news tempered the sorrow after a while when I learned that Rose's bitch had had two puppies and I was to get one of them.

Shock awaited me on the beach. It had been 're-organised' by the bureaucrats and measurers from Dalyan and most of the huts now stood in serried ranks, all painted brown and crowded together within a few feet of each other

The effect was that of a concentration camp. No more higgledy-piggledy, varicoloured, Bohemian-style shanties and no more of the gypsy atmosphere. Fortunately, my *baraka* was further down the beach and still quite isolated, but I hadn't been in residence long when a group of shaven-headed men arrived with building materials and began to erect a hut within ten feet of my bedroom. Inquiries ascertained that the men were soldiers who were building it for the Dalyan *jandarma kommutan* (commander of police). I knew him slightly and had nothing against him but didn't fancy having him in residence so near. Next day, the Old Man appeared and told me he would be moving his hut to my area. He was polite enough; but not friendly as he had once been and I also didn't fancy having him living near me. It made no difference – a couple of days later he began to move in with wood, hammers, nails and, horror of horrors, corrugated iron sheets for the roof. He chose a spot not 30 feet away from my place and set to with a vengeance, tight-lipped and censorious of mien, pounding the nails in as though he were pounding them into me. I'd rather have had two *kommutans* living next to me than one Old Man, but I'd got him and had to cope somehow. I longed for the arrival of Rose and her mother who would smooth things over, but that would not be until August. In the meantime, I did get my new puppy, Jo-Jo's daughter. The Old Man dumped her at the hut, saying with his usual grumpiness, 'You can have her, she's a girl. Her name is Findik.' I took her in and didn't change her name, which I found meant cobnut and was a very common name for dogs in Turkey. She was the colour of a nut, short-coated and had clever eyes. Soon she became my shadow, just as Jo-Jo had been.

Before long the Old Man showed up with another group of men and building materials of the cheapest kind and began to supervise the construction of their hut, 20 feet directly in front of mine on the river side, thereby obscuring the wonderful view of the delta. I was sure it wasn't coincidence that had caused him to bring them there. He was trying to box me in, but why? He began to scurry back and forth between the huts, gossiping and glaring in my direction as he had done the year before. It seemed he had not yet finished with me. Only Baki's faded blue hut with its avenue of oleanders still pleased the eye in our area.

My privacy was gone and with it some of my love for the beach. For the first time, I wanted to get away. I took long walks with Findik and went swimming, but it didn't help when I had to come back to the ugliness, the proximity of my neighbours and their noise and smells (fortunately mostly of cooking).

There was now a 500 metre no-man's-land between the channel and the nearest hut and it was rumoured that this area would be cut and dredged to make the channel much wider, facilitate the entry of boats to the river and provide a yacht marina.

Then, the Old Man who loved to bear bad news, passed word around that we would all have to leave the beach for good that year. I was in a state of flux – love the beach, leave the beach, stay, go, where, how, why, what of the delta and conservation? And, was it true? One never knew with the Old Man, who was an inventive gossip.

I went to Ortaca market and bought yards of a cheap, white material which I hung around my balcony to obscure me from the neighbours and the ever-increasing number of people (mostly men), who sneaked across the sand, peering into my windows. My white curtains ballooned out like sails when the wind freshened each afternoon, giving the *baraka* the appearance of a chunky ship under sail.

I rarely saw Abidin. He was mostly in Ekincik, where he also had his share of troubles with the local people who, jealous of his success – he now had eight boats – had cut adrift his boats and sought by various means to drive him out. One night the entire village descended upon his tent (he lived in a tent then in summer) and set fire to it. Abidin escaped into the surrounding woods and eventually made his way to one of his boats and got to Dalyan. On the way through the woods he had the incredible bad luck to be bitten by a scorpion and as a result, spent some days in the hospital at Muğla. So Abidin had his problems too, but his were not restricted to one man as mine were, he was up against an entire village . . . in fact, he took them to court and after years of litigation of an unparalleled kind (Man against Village), he won his case and never heard another peep out of Ekincik village!

Two more huts were built on my other side in the month of May. I was now surrounded and felt like the American settlers must have done when crouched behind their wagons circled by a band of marauding redskins. Though in fairness I must say that the families in the two newest huts were friendly enough and we always exchanged greetings.

In June I read in the *Turkish Daily News* that a song contest was to be held in Çesme near Izmir. It was an international competition and the public were invited to contact the organiser in Çesme. A catchy tune had been sounding in my subconscious for some time and, sitting on my deck, lying on the sand or walking with Findik I had found some words to match the tune. Now I applied myself with concentration and came up with '*Merhaba*' a song of Turkish/English friendship with a Turkish rhythm and English words. I had trained as a singer in the 50s and sung professionally. Why not enter as the British contender? I needed a change from the beach and this seemed to be a perfect opportunity. I sent off for details of the contest.

While waiting for a reply, Professor Erdal and his students came to the beach and we renewed our talks and plans for Friends of Dalyan. He had not been able to found our group officially; there were many obstacles to founding groups in Turkey and his position as professor in a university made his task more difficult. He intended to complete all the formalities that winter for he too had heard the new rumours of development of the beach and knew there was no time to lose. We and his team walked the beach and counted turtle tracks, making notes of distances, numbers of nests and of false crawls – when a turtle is not satisfied with conditions on the beach and returns to the sea without nesting.

Details of the Çesme Song Contest arrived and I set about fulfilling them. Amongst other things I needed a cassette tape of my song and a written arrangement. I phoned an old friend of mine in London, Barrie Guard, a gifted musical arranger and hummed the song to him over the phone ... could he do an arrangement for me and could he organise a studio for me in London very soon, so that I could record it? Barrie did a fantastic job and within ten days I had flown to London, recorded the song and bussed to Çesme where I met the organiser of the contest.

'You're too late,' he told me in excellent English. 'The British contender has already been chosen.'

'But there are still five days till the deadline,' I said, or rather shouted, for ten-decibel rock music throbbed about us. I handed him my tape and saw his expression brighten as he listened to it. Barrie had made a sensational arrangement with plenty of percussion in the Oriental manner, cymbals, drums, finger-bells.

'I like it,' said Ahmet, the organiser, 'but we can't use it in the con- test, as I told you, the British entrant has already been chosen.' I pointed out that I thought it unfair not to say unethical, but he was adamant. After all my enthusiasm, the efforts and the speed with which I had turned out this song, I was hugely disappointed. Ahmet called to his assistant, a long-legged Scandinavian-style beauty to play my tape on the hi-fi and the catchy, effervescent sound reverberated around us. Contestant or not, I was proud of my song. Ahmet seemed to share my enthusiasm and some of his staff over in the corner even started to dance, clicking fingers and letting go in fine Turkish style.

Ahmet invited me to sing my song as part of the Çesme Festival Week, not as contestant but entertainer. It was better than nothing, I decided. All expenses paid for a week, car at my disposal and I would perform it as part of the back-up at the televised performance of the contest finals on the last night. This confirmed my decision to accept his offer. I was sure that if my song were televised it would have a success and as an added bonus my song and I could be used to promote our campaign for Dalyan and the turtles. We were known then by a few people; but this TV appearance would put us on the map.

I returned to the sandspit, and the hut, exhilarated, refreshed. Findik had been staying at the *restoran* with Ömer during my absence and I found her well and waiting on my jetty when I got back, just as her father used to do. Soon word spread around Dalyan village and the beach that Kaptan June would sing on television the following Saturday night. They knew about my singing as I had often sung at campfires on the beach or at weddings. I did not yet know any Turkish songs by heart, but 'Summertime' 'The Skye Boat Song' and anything written by the Beatles were much requested.

So I went to Çesme. The week flew with rehearsals; my two performances at the Kale, both highly successful with the audience clapping in rhythm and joining in singing the last word – *merhaba*. In Çesme I had bought a pale blue satin ensemble of Turkish harem pants and short-sleeved blouse. The nights were incredibly hot but I hung an ostrich feather boa round my neck for added glamour. My fellow entertainers were all Turks and we got on famously. I also met all the other participants in the festival and contest. There were parties every night and I had a great time, despite the disappointment of not being able to compete. I met the British contestant, who, surprisingly, turned out to be a black South African with an Irish passport. A nice chap, he got second prize with a song written by himself. First prize went to the Turkish contestant, a charming, handsome man, already a well-known singer in Turkey. Third prize was won by the Monaco entrant with a mediocre song and less than mediocre performance, but she was a good-looker with long legs and just about out-of-school age.

Watching the show on finals night I realised how naïve I had been to think of entering this contest for obviously I was a maverick. I had thought that a good song and good voice were all that were needed, but now I saw that youth was king.

Alas, Ahmet did not keep his promise that I would sing on the television programme. I was not called for rehearsal and when I sought him he was not to be found. On the big night I was escorted to a ringside seat, for the performance which took place in a vast marquee and I felt the electricity of the audience, a well-known feeling from my performing days. This audience was a good one, ripe for that marvellous union between audience and performer that sometimes occurs, causing an energy flow, a power akin to electricity. I knew that '*Merhaba*' would have had a success, but it was not to be and I had to sit and watch an antedeluvian 'speaker' with a well-known TV face mumble on for twenty minutes about nothing of importance, as the audience deflated itself. Then came a series of poor performances from various 'artistes'. After that the contest . . .

When I got back to Dalyan the following day I learned that many people had waited up until the tune-off sign for me to appear and sing '*Merhaba*'. How could I explain? What could I do but return to the beach, keep a low profile and hope they would forget?

I threw myself back into the hedonistic beach life once more, swimming, sunbathing, enjoying the sunsets with a glass of wine, and meeting the visitors who came, some to stay with me, some day-trippers from Dalyan, some overnighters in rented huts.

Before long there was another one of those strange events that make this country the antithesis of boring – I got another stalker, but this one did not actually stalk, he lay on my deck in front of my door and when I sent him away, came back the next night and lay there again. He did me no harm and did not look alarming, in fact, he was young and rather nice looking in a delicate, waif-like way. His name was Aydin and he was an orphan, I learned from Ömer, who had nothing bad to say about him. I presumed he was another one of those young men wanting to get out of his army service or go abroad and that eventually he would propose, but it fact he didn't speak, just lay there and slept and was gone when I got up in the mornings. I did not tell Abidin on the rare occasions when I saw him, for I knew he had found the man he considered to be the right suitor for me, an ancient widower from Köyceğiz.

'Never,' I screamed at Abidin when he presented this shuffling old wreck.

'He's full of money and property. It will all be yours.'

I was appalled. How could Abidin know me so little?

One night in one of the *restorans* I met a man who was to play a vital part in the future of Dalyan. As so often happens with important things, the meeting originally had a normal impact. Glen Noble was a young man from Brixton who co-ordinated television programmes for eventual production and sold the finished concept to someone who would produce it. My story of the beach and efforts to achieve some protection for the turtles intrigued him. I lent him my Proposal for the Establishment of a National Park – Dalyan Delta. He read it and wanted to use it for a programme on conservation. I gave him a copy. A shot in the dark, but something might come of it. I knew that exposure via the media was of vital importance in attracting the support of environmentalists. Glen returned to London with my paper.

Then summer wore on and on and we began to wilt under the increasing heat. Still my stalker lay on my deck some nights when I returned from the *restoran*. One night there was a country wedding at Çandir, a hamlet that could be seen from the beach; it was perfectly placed on a hill covered with fir trees and was the place where Abidin had been born. With my then two house guests, a young English

48

couple and Kazim from the *restoran*, we set off. To my surprise, our Kaptan was my stalker, the orphan, Aydin. It was full moon and the river a masterpiece of beauty as we headed for the Çandir jetty. The first star of the evening shone splendidly above us and as though by magic, the melody of a new song began to play itself in my mind. Soon a phrase fitted into the melody and by the time we reached Çandir I had the basis of my new song – '*Star of Dalyan*'.

The wedding, held outdoors with the bride in white and the guests sitting on chairs in a circle around her whilst two musicians played drum and clarinet, was a happy affair with lots of dancing. I joined in and soon too my stalker, who turned out to be a superb dancer. Later we sailed back to the beach under the stars and moon and I had to admit to myself that I did not find my young stalker entirely unattractive. That night the beach shone white in an unearthly way as though made for magic and love.

Alas! the magic of the beach in daytime was being eroded constantly. As the road being built from Dalyan to Iztuzu (the eastern end of the beach) progressed, the 'crump' of dynamite sounded more frequently reminding one of the desecration of the forest and, as surfacing of the road progressed, more and more tractors drove along the length of the beach. Usually they carried a couple of men bound for some raki-drinking in one of the *restorans*; sometimes they bore an entire family who found it easier to attain their huts by road than by the traditional river way. I was appalled to see and hear these noisy vehicles on our beautiful beach and shuddered as they pounded over the very areas of sand where the turtle nests were.

At about that time Abidin introduced me to the governor of Köyceğiz, Mr Oğuz Berberoğlu. Köyceğiz is the county seat, encompassing Dalyan; the court of justice sits there and other official business is done.

The three of us enjoyed a good meal sitting outdoors by the river in Dalyan. I liked the governor, a charming, slightly chubby, gentleman of the old school. He spoke good English and we exchanged views about our respective countries and listened to Abidin's anecdotes about his sojourn in London when he worked as a porter in the Charing Cross area.

Inevitably the conversation turned towards future plans for the Dalyan delta and I was pleased to hear the governor declare himself in favour of protecting its beauty and natural resources. When we said goodnight he invited me to visit him in his office in Köyceğiz and made

49

me promise that I would bring him a copy of the proposal I had written for the Dalyan delta.

I went back down to the beach in an optimistic mood happy that I had support from someone powerful in our district.

There were many wrongs to be addressed on the beach and I did visit the governor to enlist his help in stopping tractors from using the beach and to get the local authorities to put out some rubbish bins. Nothing happened, but I cannot blame the governor for that, it is simply that things do not happen fast here.

In August Rose and her mother came from Istanbul and there was a happy reunion between us and the dogs, who were as delighted to see them as I was. The Old Man did not match our enthusiasm and remained cold and disapproving. I kept out of his way, but he often showed up at my gate shouting about the dogs. I must confess I had been a bit naughty and adopted another stray who had turned up on the beach. He was a handsome black and white dog of the Dalmatian type. I called him Harlequin as his markings were diamond-shaped. He never came on to the deck but lived on the sand and was a great guard. He hated roaming men and saw them off effectively. But the OM insisted I tie him up and, to keep the peace, I did so. Harley did not like that. Findik's brother, Whisky, also presented a problem in that he spent most of his time with Findik and me. This made the OM jealous. I did not want to encourage Whisky, but there were no fences on the beach, our huts were close and Whisky seemed to like our place – so what could I do?

I still had had no replies from the WWF and Brigitte Bardot to letters written the year before, or any acknowledgement from the Ministry of Tourism in Ankara to whom I had also addressed an appeal for help. But I continued to collect signatures on the petition I intended to present to Mr Özal, the prime minister of Turkey. There were more visitors in 1986 and more signatures.

Rumours continued about building at Iztuzu and across the channel, but no dredgers arrived, no bulldozers and I knew the weather as from October would make it impossible to build on the beach and so felt slightly more confident.

Chapter Nine

Exodus

And so we happy beach-dwellers passed the glorious days and sultry nights of August in wishful thinking and hopes. Bonfires, drums, music and dancing on the sand. Starlit hours on balconies drinking and laughing; then the whisper of reeds over one's head and the warm muzzle of a dog that had infiltrated the bedroom. Cool mornings following baby turtles' tracks; a velvety sea all to oneself to float on and the sensual feel of hot sand underfoot.

Occasionally a low-draught yacht would come into the river and we would make friends with their owners. Sometimes these were old friends from my sailing days on *Bouboulina*. One such, Aşik Kaptan (Kaptan in love) from Selemiye, up the coast beyond Marmaris. At Ömer's *restoran* my beribboned tambourine was passed from hand to hand, while Abdullah the waiter played the finger-bells and danced more seductively than any houri.

On the debit side . . . the Old Man's moods grew worse and this, to a certain extent, estranged me from Rose and her mother. Poor Whisky also got the force of the Old Man's moods and was chained up sometimes for days on end. This distressed me and Rose terribly and we begged for him to be freed, but the Old Man refused. I would hear the dog whimpering and see him lying in his own excrement and could do nothing during the hours of daylight, but when it was dark I often sneaked across the sand and freed him. I began to do something I never thought I'd do on that lovely beach – I began to hate.

One day Whisky wasn't there at all. He was missing for two days. I heard that the OM had sold him to someone in Ortaca. On the evening of the third day, I saw a bedraggled Whisky landed on the shore by the river in front of my jetty. He had escaped and negotiated roads, reeds, marshes and river to get back. My heart went out to him but he was soon recaptured by the OM and tied up again under their hut. The pattern repeated itself. Whisky went missing again, no doubt taken back to Ortaca, but once more he escaped and appeared on the beach some days later. I could bear his suffering no longer and hid him in my hut; it wasn't easy as it was very hot in the daytime. Then I offered via Rose to buy Whisky from the OM but he refused.

My friend, Warren, from Australia came to stay and it helped for he gave me moral support. The OM was quite friendly to him and, in the course of time, told him I was a whore and that he was about to denounce me to the authorities and have me sent away from the beach. Warren and I could only laugh at this crazy idea but, in fact, the OM did try to collect signatures from some of his pals on the beach and one night we and two other visitors to my hut were treated to the weird sight of the OM haranguing a circle of men on the sand in front of his hut and, after many threatening gestures in my direction (we four were there in full view), he waved a paper in the air and then passed it around for signing. Nothing came of this, of course, but on my next visit to the governor in Köyceğiz I complained of this nasty occurrence and he, shocked, offered to intervene on my behalf. In the event, the OM then did something so flagrant that I was forced to go to law to shut him up once and for all.

I was returning from Dalyan one day, when I spotted the OM in his boat about to leave the beach with both the dogs on board.

As we touched the jetty I called to the Old Man, 'What are you doing?' He didn't answer but started his engine. I jumped ashore and ran towards his boat, calling out to Findik, but she was tied. I reached the boat and tried to get on board to release Findik, while she howled and tugged trying to get to me. The Old Man pulled the tiller out of its socket and came at me with it raised above his head.

'I'll kill you,' he yelled, rushing at me, his face dark with rage. A small crowd had gathered by now and stood watching. Warren, who had been on the deck of the hut, now rushed out with René, an old friend and frequent visitor at the hut. Both ran towards the OM and tried to grab the tiller from him.

'I'll kill you too,' he roared, turning upon them. Then, with surprising agility, he leapt into his boat, thrust the gear lever in and moved away from the shore. In a few minutes his boat had disappeared in the tall reeds, for he had no mast on his boat and was therefore impossible to see.

I was in a state of shock. Warren and Renée too. The small group watching commented in Turkish, while Rose and her mother watched from their balcony. I cried fearing what would happen to the dogs with the OM in such a demented state. Warren, who hadn't a clue what had provoked all this, tried to console me. When I was sufficiently recovered, I went over to Rose and said, 'Can't you do something to help?'

Her eyes were troubled, sad, 'He is my father. I know he is wrong, but I can't do anything.' Mother sat nearby. She simply glared at me as though I were an enemy. My heart sank. Would I ever understand these people or they me?

After a quick consultation it was agreed that Warren, René and I would go immediately to the *jandarma* post in Dalyan. Fortunately the boat which had brought me to the beach was still there and we engaged its *kaptan* to take us to Dalyan.

Our eyes scoured the river and reeds on the way back to Dalyan, but we saw no sign of the OM's boat. A great fear preoccupied me, that the OM in his fury might harm or even kill the dogs.

The *kommutan* of the *jandarma* was surprised to see three agitated foreigners arriving in his office and was more surprised to hear that our visit had to do with missing dogs. He was a youngish man, khaki-clad with a shaven head and spoke nothing but Turkish. Cemal, the owner of a carpet shop, was called in to interpret.

'Dogs?' said the *kommutan*, looking baffled.

'Yes, they've been stolen,' I said, via Cemal.

'Stolen? Why would anyone steal a dog, let alone two?' The *kommutan*'s voice rose to a higher pitch. I had to confess I did not know why they had been stolen. I just wanted them back and quickly. I tried to explain my concern.

'In England, we love dogs,' I said.

This caused a roar of laughter from the *kommutan* and his subordinate who stood rigidly to attention by the door.

'Love dogs . . .' they giggled.

'Yes, they are part of the family.'

This caused more laughter and raised eyebrows. I was losing my patience. Perhaps they belonged to the sect I had heard tell of who believe that merely to be breathed on by a dog condemns the recipient to forty years in the fires of Hell.

Through Cemal I explained that I had had trouble with the Old Man and had been to the judge about him. I also mentioned that the governor was a friend of mine. The *kommutan* now took me more seriously and was soon barking orders at his soldiers and into his walkie-talkie phone. Cemal interpreted.

The Old Man was to be found and told that he must bring the dogs unharmed to his office the next morning.

It was getting dark. We thanked the *kommutan* and shook his hand.

'There are plenty of dogs in Turkey,' he said, 'you could always get two others.' Obviously East and West did not meet easily.

After a reviving drink and a meal at Denizati *restoran*, Warren and I went in search of a boat to take us back to the hut. We found the waif, Aydin, who sailed us unerringly along the contortions of the river without the aid of lights or moon to help, for there was none that night. I sat up on the stern next to him gazing at the panoply of stars above. Somewhere the Old Man was holding the dogs and I was troubled. A shooting star splattered earthward. I made two wishes – for peace and for the safety of Findik and Whisky.

Next morning at the *jandarma* post I had the joy of seeing both dogs full of life. They weren't exactly pleased to be held on a lead by the Old Man and tried hard to break free and rush to me. Fortunately, they failed for I don't think the *kommutan* would have welcomed their presence in his office. Abidin was now called to interpret and after some hours' discussion and many glasses of tea, I was given custody of the dogs until such time as the judge in Köyceğiz would make his decision. So we all left the *jandarma* post, the dogs pulling like crazy on their leads as though frantic to get away from Dalyan and back to the beach. The OM sulked, fumed and bombasted throughout. Several of his buddies from the beach had accompanied him on his arrival, then melted into thin air as we went in to the *kommutan*. They looked shifty and ill at ease, for most were known to me and we had never had any quarrel. Before I left to go back to the beach, one sneaked up and said, 'We like you, we have nothing against you, but he is one of *us*.'

The judge's ruling was not long in coming. The Old Man was required to sign an agreement that he would never persecute me again nor threaten nor harm me, my friends, my property. The dogs were given to me. He duly signed in the presence of Abidin and a lawyer on my behalf.

I was over the moon. Safe and free at last to live without fear in my chosen place. I thanked Abidin who had once again proved himself a good friend.

'You'd better get married anyway,' he told me and took off with élan in his speedboat bound for Ekincik.

That evening Warren and I enjoyed our sundowner on the deck watching yet another memorable performance as the great orb slid behind the mountains to the west washing the sky in vermilion.

'Why don't you marry Aydin?' he asked, just like that. 'Aydin?' I was stunned. But Warren was serious. I put forward every obstacle I could think of and he countered with every reason why it *could* work. No doubt the wine we were drinking and the magical quality of the beach also had an effect, whatever, by the end of the evening I was convinced marriage with a young man 34 years my junior of an alien culture, religion and language was not only feasible but desirable. All that remained was to pop the question!

Aydin did not hesitate when I asked him the following evening on my deck if he would like to marry me. 'Yes,' he said and gave me a kiss. It was not the first we had shared, I have to confess, for this shy, skinny, slightly effeminate young man definitely attracted me. And, as I have already noted, the beach cried out to be a haven for lovers.

Now, in contrast to the months of worry and stress I had endured with the OM and the cares concerning beach, flora and fauna, an exhilarating mood of optimism filled me and I threw myself enthusiastically into preparations for my future life with Aydin.

It was now September. Warren took charge of arrangements for our engagement party which was to be held in the attractive My Marina *restoran* in Ekincik. Warren, who has a strong instinct for the exotic, chose not only my wardrobe, but that of some of the guests and flowers were procured to wear as *leis*, while Aydin was lucky not to get a flower behind the ear. Anton, a German friend staying on the beach at the time was geared-out in a turban and also René. Warren himself wore a sarong and went barefoot. I had on my blue satin outfit worn in Çesme, all the costume jewellery I possessed and a white feather boa. Irfan, the owner of My Marina, did not blink an eye when told that Kaptan June was about to get engaged to the homeless, orphaned youth, Aydin, but set to work making the evening as romantic as possible with candlelight and 50s-style music of the schmaltzy, Perry Como variety. Naturally we chose the night of the full moon to sail off from the beach in a boat steered by one of Aydin's *kaptan* friends and two more of his macho buddies who made a striking contrast to the exotic 'friends of the bride'.

It is easy to laugh about it now but that evening was in fact one of the most magical of my not uneventful life. I am quite sure the beach cast her spell and turned us into a fairy story for just one night. Abidin danced on the table, in nothing but a pair of bathing trunks, sweating like an over-heated genie. Aydin and I danced cheek to cheek for all the world as though we were created for each other. In the small hours we sailed back across the moonlit sea to our beloved beach, to the sheltering embrace of the hut with its night sounds of reeds rustling and its heady aroma of resin rising out of the pine planks. The two dogs met us at the jetty and Billie Holiday emerged from a dark corner with arched back and glinting, yellow eyes ... like a sorceress.

Warren left reluctantly to return to Australia with many admonitions, plans for the wedding and promises to sew the seed pearls on my bridal gown.

One day some good news arrived in a letter from Glen Noble. His TV programme had been accepted and shown on Channel 2. A very small part of it had been devoted to Dalyan. I felt like a fisherman who has cast his bait and waits a bite. Little did I realise how important those few minutes' media exposure would prove to be for the Dalyan turtle campaign.

Aydin came to the beach most nights. During the day he ferried tourists about on his boat (not his own, he merely worked on it) and the last friends and tourists came and went. When my fiancé did not show up on the beach for a few nights, I got a lift in a friend's boat and went to look for him in Dalyan. I found him in a *restoran*, drunk, hanging round the neck of an obese German woman who told me they had been having an affair for the past few days. I told him I never wanted to see him again and left back to the beach. He showed up full of excuses the next day, but my interest in him and my trust were gone. I could only see him holding hands with his fat *frau* – hers looked more like a trotter than a hand! It was not too hard to give him back the ring (which I had bought anyway) but harder to forget his boyish charm and the brief happiness he had given me. I missed him on the beach and smouldered for a while. As for Aydin, he made several attempts to win me back over the next few years but finally gave up and married one of many lonely visitors who crossed his path. She whisked him off to Germany and, as far as I know, he is still there.

I now had more time for the turtle campaign. I went back to my former activities sending off letters to conservationists and getting information back. One day, the bait I had thrown with the TV nature programme got the bite I had been waiting for – a messenger (fisherman) turned up on the beach telling me a telegram awaited me at the PTT in Dalyan. I went there and found that it was from someone I'd never heard of – Keith Corbett, who asked me to phone him in

London urgently. In those days it was not easy to get a phone connection, but I did get through eventually. Keith Corbett had seen the piece about Dalyan on Channel 2 and knew that our beach was an important nesting place of the *Caretta caretta*. He was British Adviser on environmental matters at the Council of Europe and was going to a meeting in Strasbourg a week later. He wanted additional information and photos in order to be able to ask questions about the situation for the nesting turtles at that meeting. He told me that two still shots of our beach had been shown on the programme. These were photos that I had given Glen.

I rushed down to the beach, found the necessary papers and photos and returned the next day to Dalyan to send them to Keith in Strasbourg. He received them in time and was able to speak on behalf of the *Caretta caretta*.

It was the breakthrough I had hoped for for years. Keith proved to be a campaigner and champion of considerable tenacity and knowledge. He wrote me letters and introduced me through one of them to a Greek lady, who was also to prove a dedicated turtle campaigner and tireless supporter, whose name was Lily Veneselos. We then exchanged letters and as in the manner of links in a chain, she recommended that I contact a Turkish lady conservationist, Nergis Yazgan. She wrote me long, impassioned letters full of interesting information. I was now in contact with knowledgeable, useful collaborators, all of whom were keen to protect the nesting beach of the *Caretta caretta*. My life had taken on new dimensions. I was no longer a lone voice crying in the wind. I was 'in the field' in other words, living in Turkey, in Dalyan and well placed to complement the work of all these people by providing on-the-spot details. Keith was keen to come to the beach and I invited him to stay in the hut. Through Lily, Keith and Nergis, I finally came into contact with the WWF in Switzerland and exchanged letters with their director, Dr Hartmut Jungius, who invited me to visit him when I was in that country. I also kept in touch with Professor Erdal in Ankara who was delighted to hear of the Council of Europe's interest in Dalyan. I promised to visit Ankara soon.

Friends of Dalyan was still but a dream, but I hoped that that winter we could found it.

I did not know it, but in another area, the sword of Damocles was about to fall.

One day Ömer the *restoran* owner appeared at my *baraka* looking distraught.

'We all have to leave the beach,' he said. I gasped. 'When?'

'By the end of October,' he told me.

So this was it – all the rumours and the fears – here were coagulated. I asked him how he knew. He had heard the announcement over the Tannoy system in Dalyan that very day. There could be no doubt. Every hut had to be removed and at the owner's expense. No reasons were given for this edict. Ömer was a real beach-lover like me and we sat for a while discussing the bad news and commiserating with each other. The end of October was less than a month away. That night in bed I cried for another lost dream, another rape to be committed against this beautiful, natural place.

I went to see the governor just to check that the order was official and irreversible. He told me that plans were underway via the Ministry of Tourism for development of the beach. A yacht marina was planned, some hotels and *restorans* and (to my amazement) a road along the beach and 50 bungalows in the centre at a place known as Kuçuk Dalyan, where 12 huts now stood ... a beautiful place of sand dunes and oleanders adjoining a lovely lake used by the Dalko Fish Co-operative as a fish nursery. It was totally protected, no fishing was allowed there, no craft were permitted on it and there were no buildings on its shore.

The governor understood my distress at having to leave the sandspit.

'No matter what, there will always be a place for you on the beach. You belong to each other,' he said, offering me sugar for my glass of tea in his comfortable office with the portrait of the great Kemal Ataturk looking down on us from the wall.

'They will be proper bungalows, made of concrete. Strong, modern, with electricity and mains water. I will see that you are able to rent one,' he said proudly.

I was grateful for his kindness, but forbore to tell him I preferred the ramshackle *baraka*s of the beach and wanted to get away from electricity, concrete and neighbours. He showed me a plan of the complex.

'You have your place in your paradise,' he said, pointing to the phalanx of bungalows, row upon row – obviously there was a difference between the governor's idea of paradise and mine.

So I prepared to leave the beach like all the others. But Keith Corbett sent a message to me that he would be arriving with a Turkish herpatologist, Professor Remse Geldiay, in the third week of October.

They arrived in a thunderstorm as I awaited them in Dalyan. Keith turned out to be a slightly built, blue-eyed man in his early forties. Professor Geldiay white-haired and well into his seventies. He had done a series of studies of the *Caretta caretta* on this coast in the 1970s and knew more about these shy creatures and our beach than anyone. Despite torrential rain, Keith insisted on going down to the beach immediately. It was early evening and we arrived there in darkness, wet through, to fumble around in the gloom finding and lighting oil lamps and making up beds. Nothing bothered Keith and the professor; they were simply delighted to be on the beach, even in a hut in a deluge.

Next day it was bright and after breakfast they set off to explore the area, armed with binoculars and cameras.

They stayed three days in the hut and explored the beach from end to end. Keith climbed all the surrounding hills and some of the mountains too. And we talked and talked about turtles and conservation; we ate each night in Ömer's kitchen, for he was still on the beach; like me he wanted to stay until the last moment. I learned more about turtles in those three days than I could have hoped for, because Professor Geldiay was an acknowledged expert on *Caretta caretta* and other species of turtle. With students from his Izmir university he had made extensive studies in our area in the 1970s. Alas, he was no longer young and took retirement soon after his visit to the beach.

The sadness of leaving the beach affected all who had lived there. The *restoran* owners were badly hit for they also lost their livelihood. The fishermen were hard hit for they would no longer have a place to shelter on winter nights while waiting to retrieve their nets and would have to go back to Dalyan or sleep in rough conditions on their boats. Böce Ahmet, the Insect, came to see me and bemoaned the bad news. What would become of him?

My hut was constructed in such a way that it could be taken to pieces and the sections stored and so I arranged with Mehmet to take it apart, put the sections on a boat and stack them on a piece of land belonging to Arif, another *restoran* owner, who had land on the river near Dalyan.

Each day there was the nasty sound of breaking wood as some hut owner or other pulled down his once happy home. Each day the beach became more deserted. Of the *restorans* where we had danced and feasted nothing remained but a few broken chairs, some forlorn-looking oleanders and, in the case of the Istanbul *restoran*, its concrete foundations – an ugly sight on the natural spread of sand. Tayfun (Typhoon) Lightning's father and the family were some of the last on the beach.

59

I waited no longer, but packed up all my possessions and trans-shipped them on Mehmet's boat to be stored for the winter. I was leaving for some months in Europe, but intended to present my petitions to the Turkish prime minister beforehand. I did not wait to see the destruction of my beloved *baraka*, I could not bear it. The last sound I heard as we moved away from that well-known shore was the sound of a sledgehammer and the splintering of wood.

Chapter Ten

Ankara

I was pleased when Abidin said he would accompany me on my mission to Ankara. I knew from my innumerable experiences in Dalyan that the presence of a man was of inestimable worth to a lady when dealing in Turkey. Also, I would not feel lonely on this my first visit to the capital. As an added bonus, Abidin knew the prime minister's press secretary, Mr Can Pulak, a man of some influence.

We decided to leave Dalyan for Ankara towards the end of November and to stay there two or three days. In the meantime, I set about establishing myself in the tiny old cottage I had rented from Mehmet. I soon discovered that Mehmet's children were terrified of dogs, as many of the locals were, and so Findik, Whisky and Billie the Cat went to live with the mother of one of the waiters I had known on the beach. She was an animal lover and would even let them come into her house. I missed them terribly, but it was the best thing to do. Later, after Ankara, I was leaving for Greece and England and would not be back in Dalyan until the spring.

Dalyan at that time was a quiet village with a population of about three thousand. There was a mosque, a bank, several small grocery shops, many cafés full of men, a few *pansiyons* (pensions) and *restorans* and one bar. It was, of course, situated on the river and a certain number of river boats were moored along the quay. Nothing much happened in winter and the highlights of my couple of weeks spent there were the evenings when I was invited to eat with Mehmet and family or with a German/Swiss couple I had met recently who had just come to live in the village. Mehmet's wife, Fatma, a shy beauty, produced some delicious food and I was fond of her daughter Gülşa and son Mustafa, both under school age. My new foreign friends were Lily and Kuno Steuben. He was a writer and conservationist who was, paradoxically, a

61

keen hunter. Their friendship was precious to me and we passed many convivial hours eating Lily's fine cooking and talking about Dalyan, the beach, turtles and the future of this vulnerable beauty spot. Kuno told me he was in communication with the WWF in Germany and I discussed my activities with him and we agreed to exchange information, so, once more I did not feel alone in my aims. There were no other foreigners living in Dalyan at that time.

One rarely saw women outdoors in Dalyan village, unlike the easy-going beach life where there were often women and children about. Women only appeared on Saturday mornings at the market and would then stagger home laden down with kilos of fruit and vegetables, not to mention the odd chicken carried head-down with a piece of string attached to its feet. Men were everywhere; lounging in the cafés; hanging about outside the post office; buying meat at the butcher's. The atmosphere was not at all like that of the beach and I longed for my old lifestyle. Abidin had rented a house across the river from the village and was installed for the winter; he also had his office in the main street of Dalyan and I would often sit in there chatting with him.

At dinner one evening at Mehmet's, chicken was served.

'Mustafa killed it,' said Mehmet as my portion was placed in front of me.

'Killed this chicken?' I squeaked, looking warily at the piece on my plate.

'Yes. He's practising for *bayram*,' Mehmet looked proudly at Mustafa, but I surveyed the tot with new eyes. Killed a chicken ... practising for *bayram* ... that was the Islamic religious festival when rams were sacrificed all over the country. I had a vision of this chubby child, knife poised, about to slit the throat of a ram bigger than himself. I clamped my mind shut upon this vision and applied myself to eating the chicken.

The rains really began to come now in a positive deluge and it got dark at five in the afternoon. An incredible contrast with summer when we did not see rain for six months and enjoyed light from the mullah's first call at dawn till the first star appeared in the sky. The call of the mullah from the mosque never palled upon my ear, in fact, I had heard it even from the beach at times when the wind was in the right direction. A special, mystic cry evoking exotic yet primeval lands. I was enraptured by it.

Abidin and I took the night bus to Ankara – a journey of 12 hours. It was the first time I had been on a long bus ride, but he was a veteran as are many Turks. There exists a marvellous network by which a traveller can go from any one point in Turkey to any other, in reasonable comfort and cheaply. The only negative aspect is that Turks are compulsive smokers and this, my first long journey, was marred by air foul with smoke and the odour of nicotine. Abidin who does not smoke and in fact hates tobacco complained more bitterly than I did.

And so, on a piercingly cold day in late November 1986, we came to Ankara, the Turkish capital.

Our bus arrived very early in the morning at the seething, squalid-looking bus terminal ... the bays were filled with vehicles bearing names from the four corners of this big country and every type of traveller was to be seen, from soldiers in thick khaki fatigues, to country women wearing bloomers and headscarves, to neatly spruced city gents carrying briefcases. Voices roared in a cacophony of sound advertising wares, bus companies and destinations, while others shouted farewells and greetings.

Hungry and tired we got in a *taksi* (taxi) and found a hotel in the Kizilay area where many government offices are. Soon we were in our respective rooms freshening up and after a good breakfast in the dining-room busied ourselves phoning for appointments that day. Professor Erdal was most helpful, providing useful contacts, while Abidin was able to get an appointment for us with Can Pulak the prime minister's press secretary. Curious to see something of the city, I went out for a walk until it was time for us to leave for our meetings.

Though the skies were leaden and the cold bit into my exposed face till it was numb, my first impression of Kemal Ataturk's city was a good one. It was he, who in the early 1920s ordered the seat of government to be moved from Istanbul, where it had been for centuries, to Ankara, then a large-sized town. Now it was a city of three million people. I saw wide avenues, many trees and parks and rather austere-looking buildings, I supposed government ones, as well as attractively dressed shop windows; kiosks, cafés and *restorans*. I also saw something new to me in Turkey − pedestrians who waited for the green light before crossing the road, and vehicles being driven in an orderly way, not hooting at pedestrians and generally intimidating them.

When I got back to the hotel, I found that we had appointments for most of the day. Our first was at the prime minister's office, with Can Pulak. He received us warmly and was soon deep in conversation with Abidin and though my Turkish was poor I could hear that they were talking about Dalyan, turtles and conservation. A secretary brought in

63

files and I saw that there were press cuttings and photos mentioning Dalyan. I had not had the slightest idea that we and our cause were well-known in Ankara until then, but soon discovered that my letter to Mr Turgut Özal and the appeal signed by hundreds of people that I had sent had not gone unnoticed.

We were not able to meet the prime minister during our stay as he was leaving imminently for the United States to undergo heart surgery, but were promised an interview later in the year should we come back to Ankara.

Through Can Pulak we were then sent to the Ministry of Agriculture and Forestry, a very important ministry responsible also for National Parks in Turkey. There we were also warmly received by the director of National Parks, and after an interesting talk about the Dalyan delta were given lunch in the ministry dining-room, followed by coffee in the director's office where photographs of Köyceğiz lake and a magnificent aerial photo of our beach, hung on the walls. It was wonderful to see 'home' here but even more so to hear that this ministry was all in favour of National Park status for the Dalyan delta and had, indeed, tried to achieve it some ten years before. No reason was given for the failure of this plan.

'The time is ripe to try again,' the director told us as we left for our next appointment.

Abidin and I got in a taxi in high jubilation and headed for our next meeting which was again at the prime minister's office. This time we were to meet his righthand man and adviser on special subjects – Dr Adnan Kahveci.

We were given security tags at the entrance and escorted down miles of carpeted corridors lined with imposing-looking doors until we stopped at one and were shown into a high-ceilinged, plushly furnished room. Dr Kahveci stood up to greet us. I recognised him in any case for he was a well-known political figure in Turkey and I had seen his picture in the newspapers.

'You are causing quite a stir in Ankara,' he said smiling, 'Caretta caretta is becoming a national issue.'

Dr Kahveci motioned us to a circle of leather armchairs and called for tea and coffee. I was mightily impressed with the way we were being received by this extremely important man, especially in regard to my being a foreigner. I tried to imagine a similar scene in Whitehall with a Turkish protagonist playing my role and could not imagine it happening like this.

64

For an hour or so we talked about Dalyan, turtles, conservation. Dr Kahveci had studied and lived in the United States and was well informed on environmental matters – a rare subject until then in Turkey but obviously growing in importance if our reception in Ankara was anything to go by.

I was concerned that we still had not got an appointment at the Ministry of Tourism and told Dr Kahveci so. He did not seem surprised,

'Don't you know that the minister, Mr Mesut Yilmaz, has been quoted in the press as saying – "We cannot prejudice our tourist industry for a handful of turtles".'

I had heard the report though had not actually read it. Abidin spoke:

'How do you feel about that, sir? Can you see our beautiful Turkish coast as another Costa Brava?'

'Indeed not, we want selective tourism for certain areas and Dalyan is one of them. We've seen the disaster that is occurring in Marmaris through hurried, unsuitable development.' Abidin and I agreed with him in unison – we had seen it and were shocked.

We talked about other aspects of protection of the turtle and I mentioned Zakynthos in Greece, where many of the species had been killed or scared away due to unbridled building on the actual beaches there. He knew about it and said, 'We intend to do better here.'

'Do you think the Dalyan delta could become a National Park?' I asked, as we were on the point of leaving.

'We are sympathetic to the idea,' he answered, then added, 'or even better, an SPA (Specially Protected Area). Mr Özal favours that solution.'

It was the first time I had heard the term SPA. I was thrilled to hear the prime minister's name mentioned in connection with a specific support for Dalyan.

We spent the rest of the afternoon visiting another important environmentalist – Dr Musaffer Evirgen, adviser on Environment to the prime minister – at that time Turkey did not have a minister of Environment, or indeed a ministry.

We talked of many aspects of pollution, conservation measures and environmental problems with this most interesting man and two of his collaborators.

'What do you think of our pollution here in Ankara?' he asked me. I was careful in my reply for I did not want to offend him, nor his country where we had been so politely received...

65

'It's no worse than many other cities of the world,' I said, though I had to add that my chest, sensitive to smog, felt on the verge of bronchitis after some time spent in the sulphur-smelling air.

'Lignite,' said Dr Evirgen. 'It was banned in London some years ago, with spectacular results. We are installing natural gas brought by pipeline from Russia. In time, all of Ankara will have clean air. Then we can start worrying about vehicle pollution . . .'

On leaving, he gave me his card and told me to contact him with news about Dalyan.

It was dark and beginning to rain when we came out on to the street. We hailed a passing cab, jumped in and set off for the offices of *Cumhuriyet*, one of Turkey's leading newspapers.

Cumhuriyet's headquarters provided a contrast to the restrained atmosphere of the offices we had visited so far. People rushed back and forth; phones rang incessantly and there was a press of people crowded into a series of what looked more like compartments than rooms. We were shown into the office of the chief news editor and, after a chat with him, were passed on to a reporter in another office; after being interviewed about ourselves and Dalyan, we went to the photographic studio where we were photographed for the next half an hour.

We got back to the hotel, tired but elated, and changed quickly in time to go out to dinner with Professor Erdal.

Next morning there was a press conference in our hotel; this lasted all morning and we were subsequently the subject of articles in several daily papers, including the English-language one – the *Turkish Daily News*; they gave us and the turtles a whole spread with photos.

In the afternoon we were asked to go to the TRT offices (Turkish Radio and Television) where we were interviewed by reporters from the News Desk.

That evening Abidin left for Dalyan. I stayed on until the next day and spent that evening again talking far into the night with Professor Erdal and some of his students, already friends from the beach. Everyone was shocked to learn that all the *barakas* had been removed. In fact, the ODTU hut was still there; it was the only one permitted to stay and that because their scientific studies were not yet complete. Professor Erdal was passionately fond of the Dalyan area and had taken some of the best photographs ever of beach, delta, village. He was a photographer of quasi-professional level and had had a number of exhibitions.

Everyone was elated about our successful visit to Ankara.

We talked again about Friends of Dalyan, in fact our plans for founding the group had been reported in the press. We did not see that anything could now prevent our going ahead with it.

Ominously, the ministry of Tourism had not given us an appointment. Was it that they did not want to know about us, I wondered. On a personal level I was delighted to have been welcomed everywhere else in Ankara, taken seriously, not dubbed a crank, and with no attempt being made to control me, unlike the situation in Dalyan.

On 28 November, a taxi drove me to the airport through Ankara's sober streets under a menacing sky. I was flying to Athens to meet another turtle lady whom I as yet knew only by letter, Lily Veneselos.

My mind raced over the eventful two days spent here. Abidin and I had brought to Ankara an impassioned plea for the protection of a species; a remote place of outstanding beauty and its flora and fauna.

I pictured the minister of Tourism, Mesut Yilmaz, all-powerful in his office – that power emphasised by the fact that touristic development enjoyed top priority in this country … and I knew that we had a formidable opponent.

What would be the outcome?

Chapter Eleven

Building

The meeting with Lily Veneselos in Athens added new dimensions to my role as a turtle champion. She was already an experienced campaigner for *Caretta caretta*; capable, informed and well connected. She had won her spurs with several years of efforts to protect the *Caretta* at Laganos on Zakynthos, one of the most important *Caretta* nesting beaches in the Mediterranean. By comparison, our beach at Dalyan stood a distant second. At that time Zakynthos still counted turtle nestings and hatchings in the region of almost 2,000 per season, whereas the Dalyan nestings that we had been able to assess roughly from Professor Geldiay's studies of the 1970s were thought to be 300 to 400 per season. Despite Lily's considerable efforts and dedication, the situation in Zakynthos was deteriorating, largely due to inadequate government intervention and the insensitivity and greed of local 'developers'. It was just the scenario I feared might befall Dalyan's turtles unless we could get immediate protective support from the Turkish government. Hence, it was impossible to overestimate the importance of my meeting with Lily.

The day after my arrival, I was invited by Lily to a press conference at the headquarters of the Hellenic Society for the Protection of Nature. Lily, a petite, dark-haired and dynamic lady in her early fifties, welcomed me like an old friend. Before the journalists arrived she told me of her hopes that a joint collaboration between herself and me, on behalf of both Greek and Turkish turtles, could have a positive effect for all concerned.

Four of Greece's leading journalists came to the press conference. I was questioned about my visit to Ankara and replied that I had had an encouraging time there and had been assured that the Turkish government considered environmental issues to be important. Asked whether the Greek island of Zakynthos had been mentioned, I said that indeed it had and by no less than the Turkish prime minister's special adviser, Dr Adnan Kahveci.

Lily, who was disenchanted with the Greek minister of environment over his failure to implement measures to protect the turtles at Laganos, took this opportunity to say to the press that it was to be hoped the Greek government would in future take a view as enlightened as that of the Turks.

Next day the Greek papers were full of articles and photos of turtles and Lily and I were both quoted. Later I got a telephone call from the Turkish embassy asking me to give an interview to the Athens correspondent of the Turkish daily *Miliyet*. I agreed and the following day a front-page article with photo appeared in *Miliyet* in Turkey. Friends of Dalyan was also mentioned for I had taken the opportunity to give an added booster to our plans. All in all the press had been marvellous and Lily and I were delighted and sure turtles and conservation issues in both countries would benefit. I could only marvel that, given the tense situation then existing between Greece and Turkey vis-à-vis Cyprus we had encountered nothing but harmony and goodwill.

A few days later, I flew to London where I stayed with friends. During my two-months' stay in England I saw Keith Corbett several times. An interview was arranged with BBC Radio 2 in which Keith, Lily and I participated. Keith was with Societas Herpatologica and acted as their observer at the Council of Europe's environmental meetings. Sea turtles, endangered worldwide, were often on the agenda. Through Keith and Lily I was now introduced to another link in the chain of turtle champions – Günther Peter, a German.

Our first contacts were of the same kind as those I had originally had with Keith and Lily – by letter and telephone. Günther, an engineer by profession, had come to turtle conservation in a similar manner as I had, only his indoctrination was more dramatic. On holiday with his wife in the 1970s he had witnessed the slaughter of hundreds of Green turtles on a beach in the Philippines. This brutal sight had so disturbed him that he set about finding a way to stop the massacre. In Germany he founded a conservation group called Aktion Gemeinschaft Artenschutz. It now had many thousands of members affiliated with other organisations worldwide.

Soon my ever-increasing mail was augmented by letters and printed matter from Germany. Günther was also a great telephoner and often called me with advice, news and admonitions. I was careful of my use of the phone to call anyone and preferred to write letters. My finances were limited and all my expenses to do with the turtles came out of my own pocket.

Nergis Yazgan had kept up a correspondence with me ever since our introduction to each other via Lily Veneselos some months before. Nergis was president of an Istanbul-based group called Doğal Hayati Koruma Derneği (Wildlife Care Foundation). She was also a tireless, enthusiastic campaigner for protection of nature. She spoke excellent English (we had spoken on the phone in Turkey) and DHKD had an office in Istanbul with a handful of helpers. Their membership count in those days was around 300. Conservation was a new concept in Turkey, but the turtles and Dalyan were about to put it on the map and Nergis was to become an important figure in the environmental picture in Turkey.

And so the winter passed quickly for me and, on 27 February, I returned to Dalyan.

Once back in the village I began to look around for a house of my own, for Mehmet's tiny cottage was but a temporary haven. More importantly, I could not have my pets there and missed them terribly.

I wanted to buy something, not rent, for Dalyan and the turtles were now part of my life.

'You are one of us,' said my friend, Mehmet the Grocer, and, if I'd had any doubts about settling here, that dispelled them.

It did not take long to find my house or rather, my ruin ... for it was a tiny, derelict cottage that had not been lived in for many years. But it looked so endearing and in need of tender, loving care, dwarfed by several tall trees towering above it, that I knew it was the home for me.

I engaged a lawyer friend from Marmaris to come and negotiate for me and within a couple of weeks had bought it. It was some ten minutes' walk from the centre of Dalyan, in a quiet area of cotton fields and farmhouses. The garden of about half an acre was a wilderness of unpruned fruit trees; vines gone wild; hedges; weeds and wild flowers. Green, wild, colourful, natural, a delight to the eye.

I found a builder and began to restore the old cottage. Later there would be an addition, to house my many friends when they came visiting. I did not engage an architect for I had seen the hideous, unsuitable new constructions that were beginning to mar the village

70

and did not want to end up living in such a monstrosity. One of the workers on my cottage, a mason, not from Dalyan but from somewhere near Denizli, could speak German and he soon became my interpreter and righthand man. He was a tireless worker, resourceful and intelligent. Ibrahim Erik (Plum) was his name. Although we did not part on the best of terms when he finally went four years later, I know that without him the house would never have become the one I now love. For that I am grateful.

The hut, removed from the beach and stacked in a field by the river, was now brought by boat and tractor to my garden and installed by Ibrahim. A few days later I moved into it and the dogs and cats came home. Findik was pregnant and soon produced three gorgeous puppies, despite the fact that Whisky, her brother, was their father. I gave away two to caring local people and kept a boy, whom I named Sandy.

A lot of the old beach trophies were trotted out to decorate it and the balcony – shells, stones, gourds and the bells that had rung joyously responding to the sea breeze. Even the pots and tin cans containing geraniums had survived, thanks to the kindness of Fatma who had watered them during my absence. The ultimate survivor, the pampas grass, was planted in the water of a small stream which flowed through the garden. We were 'home' once more.

Ibrahim and a team of *ustalar* (workmen) began restoring the cottage and laying the foundations for the new part of the house. I was on the spot to comment on the way I wanted things. Mostly I left them to their own devices but one detail I did insist upon repeatedly,

'Don't let me see any concrete when it's finished. I want it to look *old*.'

They thought I was mad. Concrete was taking over Dalyan village and was regarded as visible proof of modernity and affluence. When I decided to keep the original walls of the old part of the house, the *ustalar* were horrified. How could anyone live with wattle-and-daub walls, particularly a rich foreigner? I let them do a bit of reinforcing with old bricks and that appeased them slightly. In passing, I am not rich at all, but local belief is that all foreigners are.

The building went ahead and I settled into village life. I enjoyed my friendship with Lily and Kuno and sometimes drank tea or a beer with former neighbours from the beach. The Insect was working as a tractor driver and had abandoned his unique baseball cap for a trilby hat. He also wore shoes and seemed to have some difficulty walking in them. Ömer had gone back to being a carpenter. Arif had opened a *restoran* on the river near Caunos. The Old Man had bought an ancient iron ship with a tall funnel, which soon earned the nickname with visitors of *The African Queen*. High on its stern stood another funnel, attached to a Heath Robinson-style barbecue. This contraption was for grilling meat and fish and rows of metal benches lined the deck, all this intended as a floating *restoran* for the yachties who came to Ekincik. Abidin had apparently taken leave of his senses temporarily and joined the OM as partner in this amazing venture.

The days, weeks and months passed and my house began to be recognisable as such.

Each day I found mail in my post box from various environmental agencies and conservationists. Telephoning was difficult, if not impossible and I quite often went by bus to Köyceğiz, a 35-kilometre journey, to avail myself of the phone there as they had a few more lines than we had.

In April I went briefly to Switzerland where I had business to attend to. My furniture had been in store in Lausanne since I had sold my chalet six years before and I was going to have some sent to Turkey and the rest sold. My finances were shaky and I needed capital to pay for my house. I hadn't been back in Dalyan more than 24 hours when Keith Corbett managed to get me on the phone at Mehmet's shop. He had some incredibly bad news:

'Building starts on a holiday village complex at Iztuzu beach tomorrow.'

'Tomorrow?' Could I have heard right? the lines were notoriously poor in Dalyan...

'Are you sure?' I asked, 'there is no sign of anything happening here in the village.'

'Günther phoned me from Germany, it seems some German company is involved in the building.'

I was speechless, hardly the thing to be when someone is on the other end of the line.

'Are you there?' yelled Keith.

'Yes. I'm here. What can I do?'

'Check it out and call me back as soon as you can.' Goodbyes and we hung up.

There was no sign of any imminent preparation for building of any kind in the village. I asked a few people, no one had heard the news. I was baffled.

Next day, 4 April, was one of those perfect, cloudless spring

72

mornings. I walked into the village with Whisky and Findik. Overnight a transformation had occurred. Town hall, post office and bank were festooned with flags; banners stretched across the main street with slogans proclaiming in Turkish: 'Welcome ODTU. Welcome Ministry of Tourism. Welcome Honoured German Guests.'

The streets were full of people and apparently the schoolchildren had been given the day off, for the school was closed, and many children waving flags were to be seen.

At the junction of the main street and the Iztuzu road, in front of the town hall a huge sign in Turkish and German announced the building of an 1,800-bed holiday village at Iztuzu beach, under the direct patronage of the ministry of Tourism; builders – IFA Group (German) Kavala Group (Turkish); Financing – DEG (German).

Reading the sign I now understood why we had not been received at the ministry of Tourism in Ankara. I also knew why today's events had been planned with secrecy. Once more I felt the ministry's power.

A crowd was gathering in the streets and I sat down outside the Sofra café to watch. Kuno joined me. He was apparently as astonished as I, but had heard a rumour:

'They are going to have the foundation-stone laying ceremony down at Iztuzu beach. Do you want to come?' He had been offered a lift to the beach in a *dolmuş* (minibus) and I accepted to go along . . . but first there were things to be seen here – a parade was forming, children marching in rows waving flags; the high-school band started up with their usual inaccuracy of pitch; the mayor and councillors dressed unusually in suits, ties, shoes and socks led the parade coming towards us. Mesut Yilmaz walked beside them smiling and waving to the crowd; the Vağli of Muğla walked beside him on one side and the governor of Köyceğiz (no longer my friend, he had been transferred). Applause broke out and then I saw Professor Erdal in the next row of marchers with several foreign-looking people, whom I presumed to be the German contingent. All swept by and were soon piling into various official and unofficial cars for the drive to the beach. Off went the cavalcade. We found our minibus and followed.

My mind was in a turmoil. What was Professor Erdal doing with these people? How had it all been planned without any news of it leaking out? What hope had we conservationists in the face of this *fait accompli*?

Questioned, all Abidin would say was, 'This is my country, say one thing, do another. There is no hope. It will always be like this.'

It was becoming very hot and I was glad I was wearing lightweight trousers and a T-shirt. I felt for the 'protocol' once we got down to the beach . . . they looked uncomfortable and ridiculous in their city gear.

On the way to Iztuzu I had had more shocks, seeing the evidence of the dynamiting that had been going on for the past two years. The forest was destroyed in a great swathe for most of the 11 kilometres and stone quarries, which had not existed before, now scarred many places. It looked as though a war had been fought there. I had not travelled along this road for many months and was saddened and maddened to see the desecration; tree trunks snapped in half lying by the side of the road; mounds of red earth and rock everywhere; earthmovers shoving and wrenching at new areas of forest. How many wild things had died here or fled? I thought of our visit to the ministry of Forestry and their declared aim of creating a National Park here. They were the custodians of all forests in Turkey. How had this desolation been achieved? Surely it would have needed their permission, for according to law, no one could as much as cut a branch in the forest without the ministry's permission.

The scene on the beach was so totally alien to that natural place that one could only gasp in astonishment. A phalanx of yellow bulldozers and earthmovers was formed around a wooden dais on which stood the most important members of the throng. A microphone had been erected on the dais and the mayor was introducing the minister of Tourism, Mesut Yilmaz. I could not understand all of his speech but got the gist of it. Applause followed from the crowd around the platform – men in boiler-suits and hard hats; villagers; chauffeurs, hangers-on and a sprinkling of tourists wearing bathing suits – a motley gang. With an excellent view from the top of a sand dune, I had taken off my shoes and was enjoying the feel of hot sand underfoot. In the distance I could see a bevy of cement-mixers and a row of Nissen huts, these no doubt to house the building workers. To the left stretched the magnificent sweep of sand and in the foreground was a small lake where a colony of egrets usually lived. There was no sign of them today.

I watched Mesut Yilmaz hand over the microphone to the next speaker, Herr Horst Schneider, president of the German company IFA and thought of the remark attributed to the minister in the press – 'tourism takes precedence over a few tortoises'.

Herr Schneider spoke in German which I could understand well. He spoke of his company's success in the building of hotels in the Canary Islands. As he did so, I saw in memory the ghastly ranks of high-rise buildings which had engulfed those once beautiful islands . . . I had been there on a cruise ship.

He said that this was his company's first venture in Turkey and that more touristic complexes were planned in the future. 'With our economic weight we will help these poor people,' he said, gesturing in the direction of the audience. His patronising message embarrassed me for my Turkish friends, most of whom were not looking for a handout. Indeed the standard of living then prevailing on the Aegean coast was not that of a Third World country as Herr Schneider now described it.

The blonde lady took over the microphone when he had finished speaking. She was a member of the German parliament, Frau Ingeborg Hoffmann, and now proceeded to spout a lot of figures and facts. The head of the German government agency responsible for the financing of the project then took over with more numerical facts – 40,000,000 Deutsch marks, 1,800 beds . . . she rambled on as the heat seared our heads under the noonday sun. Frau Hoffmann was handed a trowel and a spot of cement and two stones were symbolically stuck together.

The VIPs were now escorted to a spot near the sea where luncheon was to be served al fresco. This was no mean feat on a beach which had no facilities whatsoever, no electricity, water or any building. A team of waiters had been brought (I later learned) from a hotel in Marmaris. They looked stylish if incongruous in this natural setting, wearing dinner jackets and white gloves. One did not dare to think of the sweat that must have been pouring off them as they scurried back and forth serving food and drink to the fifty or so VIPs who were seated at tables on top of a concrete foundation, a ruin left over from a former beach *restoran*.

Kuno approached me. 'What do you think of this?'

'Terrible,' I said. 'But we haven't given up, have we?'

I knew that I hadn't and was determined to send a telegram to Dr Jungius in Switzerland, head of the WWF. I would enlist his help.

Kuno looked at me closely saying, 'Maybe you haven't but I intend to be careful. We are foreigners, we could get in trouble interfering.' He had a point, I knew, but I was not too worried for I knew that many Turks shared our desire to protect nature. But, I began to think that Kuno was perhaps not as impassioned so I said nothing about the telegram.

I was about to leave the beach to these visiting aliens when an even more alien sound reached my ear. For some seconds I listened in disbelief to what sounded like an alp horn and then, as I turned back towards the luncheon scene, I saw a man in *lederhosen* and Tyrolean hat playing that very instrument. I stared in amazement. What followed managed to cap this Disneyesque scene – four blonde youths and four blonde maidens dressed in Bavarian national costume now appeared and began to dance, weaving in and out of each other and linking arms swinging, while the alp horn continued its dirge and the young performers let forth an occasional yodel. Suddenly loudspeakers crackled into life and Bavarian beer-hall music added to the cacophony.

I stood on my sand dune and laughed myself almost into tears. It was as though a Fellini film crew and a *Sound of Music* one had somehow got mixed up on Iztutzu beach.

A television crew had been filming throughout and reporters were milling about. One approached me asking if I was the 'turtle lady'. He proceeded to ask me personal questions about my lifestyle in Dalyan. Did I favour Turkish men? Was I considering marrying one?

'Turtles are on my mind, not men,' I told him. And leaving him standing, went off to find transport back to Dalyan and the post office.

The last sound I heard as my minibus took off was the mournful wail of the alp horn; my last sight of the beach was of an infinite stretch of pristine beach in one direction and a blur of absurdly miscast humanity imposing itself on the other.

I wondered if any individual down there had given a thought to the *Caretta caretta* on whose beach they were intruding and wondered too if anyone among them had considered that a cry for protection of this beach had gone up and that that cry had been echoed and would not be easily silenced.

In Dalyan at the PTT I sent my telegram to the director of the WWF headquarters in Gland, Switzerland. It said simply:

'Building of 1,800-bed holiday village begun on Iztuzu beach today. Help, help, help.' June Haimoff Dalyan.

Chapter Twelve

Shifting Sands

Inevitably the ceremony at Iztuzu attracted a lot of publicity. One item in the press caused a minor furore in Turkey. His Royal Highness, Prince Philip, Duke of Edinburgh, had sent a telegram to Turkey's prime minister, asking for his intervention in delaying the building project at Iztuzu so that an environmental impact study could first be made. This request came from the Prince in his capacity of president of the WWF. I hugged this piece of news to myself. The request had certainly come in reaction to my cry for 'help' sent to Dr Jungius at the WWF.

I knew that worldwide pressure from Greens and conservationists was vital to our campaign and the media held the key to relaying this message to the public. The chain of events which had been set off by my two-minute piece shown on BBC 2 some months earlier, was proof.

Unfortunately some of the publicity rubbed off adversely on me. Some days later it was reported in a lurid Turkish newspaper that Kaptan June, a foreign lady with an interest in young men, was considering marrying a Turk. Nothing was said about my interest in turtles.

Dalyan grew in newsworthiness. One day as I got off my bicycle in the village, I was called to join the mayor, Ali Gün, for an interview by a *Cumhuriyet* journalist. *Cumhuriyet* was subsequently to be of positive help in its exposure of Dalyan's chicaneries.

Ali Gün and I sat in the bright sunlight on the village square and the reporter fired his first question at me – 'Are you against tourism?' The mayor fidgeted next to me, lighting a cigarette.

'No. I am a tourist myself.'

The reporter addressed me again: 'Are you a member of any political party?' I wondered what he was getting at.

'No,' I told him, 'politics is one of the few subjects which does not interest me.'

'Why are you campaigning for the turtles?' I spoke of my love of nature, my years on the beach and my admiration for this 'paradise', Dalyan.

The interview continued in Turkish, between the mayor and the journalist and ended with my saying once more that I was *for* tourism provided it respected the nature and tradition of the host country.

During the next few weeks more and more journalists came to Dalyan. Activity to do with the building at Iztuzu also increased. Each day lorries and other heavy vehicles roared through the village on their way to the beach. Many were loaded with gravel, for a large ramp was being built on the actual sand, so as to facilitate parking and manoeuvring of vehicles. The ground shook in Dalyan as these leviathans hurtled by and, as the weather grew drier, clouds of dust thrown up by their wheels, enveloped all. I shuddered for us and for the beach. The first in-depth reporting for the foreign press came from the English daily – the *Independent*. I was contacted by Metin Munir, their Istanbul-based correspondent. He arrived in Dalyan and we met in a café in the village.

I was new to interviews and somewhat nervous and the first question put to me surprised me somewhat: 'Do they like you in the village?'

How to answer? I knew that some liked me and some, since the advent of the turtle campaign, didn't, so I told him, 'I don't think I'm generally unpopular in the village.'

'If you were disliked, who would it be by?'

'Those who do not understand my conservationist views and those who want to get rich quickly from tourism; they would not like me.'

Metin Munir spoke perfect English. A slim man, in his late thirties, dressed in a stylish, casual way, his manner was calm and despite his tricky questions, I began to feel at ease with him.

He said, 'I must confess I already know something about you, but I was testing to see whether your version of yourself tallies with mine. I arrived last night and have talked to quite a few of the locals about you. On the whole they seem to like you.'

I was pleased to hear this, for I regarded myself as part of the scenery and had no argument with the village.

Metin Munir stayed longer in Dalyan than the other correspondents had done, in fact, he was there three days, appointed me his guide, rented a boat and spent each day exploring the delta, taking photographs and interviewing a wide variety of people. I enjoyed the time spent with this intelligent, amusing man, even though his forecast of Dalyan's future was pessimistic:

'Never will you be able to stem the tide of mass tourism. You may win the beach for the turtles temporarily, but this place is too beautiful and eventually it will be raped.'

He had loved the beach from his first sight of it but was appalled by the ravages occurring at Iztuzu and the two concrete toilets (newly built) which sprouted out of the sand like sore thumbs, blighting the channel end of the sandspit.

Almost daily there were articles in the Turkish press about Dalyan. The locals were delighted by this focus of attention, though baffled as to the reasons. No one had ever thought about turtles, except a few fishermen who regarded them as a menace to their nets and competitors for their fish catches. In the rest of the country there was bewilderment too, for conservation was a new subject and the conflict between turtles and hotel building was cause for much humoristic reporting and cartoons. But when it became known that the prime minister himself had expressed his preference for turtles over tourists, the public began to take them more seriously and enlightened journalists, like Deniz Som of *Cumhuriyet* gave increasing support to environmental protection.

Soon another link in the chain of turtle champions arrived in Dalyan – Nergis Yazgan, president of the DHKD in Istanbul.

I was delighted to meet her at last, for we had been corresponding for some months about Dalyan and had spoken on the phone a couple of times. We got on famously from the start and were inseparable for the few days she spent in Dalyan. Though 20 years my junior, Nergis seemed to me like a sister. We were interviewed for the Turkish daily *Güneş* and appeared together in a photo on the front page, she with windswept hair, me in my safari hat, on the beach, as though in our element. Nergis, a very attractive blonde, spoke excellent English and German; she had been involved for some years in guiding her smallish non-governmental organisation towards a more important, influential status quo. The Dalyan story had thrust her and her group into the forefront of conservationist activity in Turkey and she was a passionate spokeswoman for her cause and ours.

Nergis, like me, loved to swim and to walk barefoot on the beach. We covered the distance from Iztuzu to the channel several times, talking and planning without cease; dressed in shorts or bathing suits, a happy team.

At about the same time, another Turk of some importance in the environmental field came to Dalyan. Dr Tanzu Gurpinar, an ornithologist of repute, was Turkish representative to the Council of Europe, on Environment, in other words, the Turkish counterpart of Keith Corbett.

Dr Gurpinar roamed the beach and marshes for days recording sightings of many species of bird. The report which he subsequently wrote and published could only add to the urgency for protection for the entire Dalyan delta. In the matter of a few weeks he had noted the presence of over 140 species of bird.

Nergis left and I missed her lively presence and her enthusiasm. I was alone now to care about our plans and to hope.

My life was hectic, in any case, for building was going on daily on my house. The dogs and cats (now three of each) needed attention and my correspondence became ever more important as well as the phone calls which had to be made despite the many electricity cuts. But Ibrahim was doing a good job and soon I was able to move out of the hut into the restored, old part of the house. The hut, with its graffiti, wind-sock, gourds, bells and murals, still harboured me at times. I would go over there to sleep ... pretending I was back on the beach once more.

Many strangers were appearing in the village. They were easy to spot, for there were so few inhabitants, everyone knew everyone else. I rarely saw Abidin as summer wore on; he was in Ekincik or escorting his clients on the river trip. Of course, I went frequently to the beach, usually by boat, as I hated the devastation at Iztuzu and on the road. As to the Turkish people who used to go to the beach, at Iztuzu it was now forbidden to them. Guards patrolled the area and warned them off.

Kuno and Lily had become cold towards me. I did not know why, but they weren't the only ones. Some of the villagers who had been friendly, now did not greet me or were not as warm as they had been. The village was beginning to take sides – hotel or turtles – as simple as that. I was sad about Lily and Kuno and when she shouted at me one day in the street, 'don't come to our house, Kuno doesn't want you,' I was angered.

One day I confronted him at the post office, asking to know why this had been said. I did not get an explanation. All he would say was, 'We are foreigners. We don't want any trouble.'

'But many Turks also support conservation,' I said. He looked down at me from his one metre ninety-five as though I were a microbe.

'We don't want to be involved,' he said ... and walked off.

An amazing statement was made at about that time by Mesut Yilmaz. 'There are no turtles at Iztuzu. I was there and I didn't see any.' I suppose no one told him they only land at night. Other inaccuracies figured in this 'statement' including a claim that the holiday village would miss the turtles by six kilometres. If he had not been such an important man, we conservationists might have laughed.

An army of engineers, experts and technicians came to the village. I met some of them, in particular, the chief engineer in charge of construction and Kavala's chief architect, Cemal Mutlu, a charming young man with whom I became quite friendly. The engineers were mostly German and soon Kuno and Lily were to be seen with this group of hotel people.

One day a press report quoted Kuno as saying that no *Caretta caretta* turtle had nested at the Iztuzu end of the beach for ten years. When Keith Corbett heard this, he called me and Negris.

'Who is this man?' he asked. 'What does he know about it?'

Good questions which I echoed, as did Nergis. What indeed had inspired Kuno to say this? 'He's a friend, living in Dalyan,' I said.

'Some friend.' Keith's voice rose an octave. I was puzzled. Why had Kuno made such a statement publicly? He was meant to be a conservationist, but this statement played into the hands of the developers. It was another of those mysteries that emerged about that time. Professor Erdal was another. He came sometimes to Dalyan but was not as close to me as before. Friends of Dalyan was never mentioned. I supposed that his position was equivocal as Günther had unearthed the information that Professor Erdal and his team had been responsible for the engineering surveys done at the beach on behalf of the hotel planners.

I had not yet met Günther, though we had spoken on the phone and I had received many letters and much information from him. He came to Dalyan in May with a German photographer. Günther turned out to be a bouncy, cherub-faced man in his mid-forties, another impassioned, dedicated saver of nature. The three of us rented a boat and went down to the beach on a mission. Günther was so outraged by Kuno's claim that no turtles had nested at Iztuzu for ten years he wanted to visit the beach at night and prove otherwise. A veteran turtle campaigner in many countries, he was well-informed and believed Professor Geldiay's observations about this beach and its turtles to be more reliable. So we went in the late afternoon. It was a warm night and I stayed at the channel end of the beach, while they went off to Iztuzu with their cameras. Some hours later they came back triumphant. They had found a *Caretta caretta* digging her nest at Iztuzu within sight of a bulldozer and had taken several photos of her. One of these was printed in the press in Germany. So much for Kuno's statement.

Günther and Rolf, the photographer, stayed a few days. They were excellent companions and I learned much from them. Both fell in love with the delta and went back to Germany even more determined to help.

Germany was of course a key figure in the hotel construction and on the environmental level also.

The German Green party had a strong voice in German politics at that time; they were soon in touch with Günther and with us in Dalyan. As a result of their intervention something significant happened, something that was to give a huge, helping hand to our campaign. Günther discovered that the investment for the hotel building which was coming via a German financing group, DEG, was money provided by German tax-payers. Soon the Green parliamentarians were asking in the Bundeshaus an embarrassing question: 'Should German tax-payers' money be used to fund the building of a hotel in Turkey, to desecrate that part of the coast and to destroy the nesting beach of the *Caretta caretta* turtles?' A vote in the Bundeshaus decided that the money should not be advanced. We conservationists cheered and awaited the repercussions which were sure to occur as a result.

Another victory came at about that time. In response to pressure, particularly from the German Greens, night-time building was stopped at Iztuzu. This was a huge relief to us, for we were now well into the month of May and the nesting turtles had begun to arrive. It is not hard to imagine their plight when confronted by machinery, people, noise and strobe lights on arrival. Panic would have ensued and many clutches of eggs would have been jettisoned in the sea. The builders also agreed to turn off their powerful lights during the nesting and hatching period which would last until the end of September. In fairness it must be said that Kavala Grup, the Turkish construction firm working at Iztuzu, co-operated in some degree with the conservationists.

In the daytime, however, building went on apace at the site and the area now resembled a bomb-scarred place. The foundations of the hotel itself were being laid at the eastern end of a brackish lake, the one where a colony of egrets used to preen their elegant whiteness. Part of the lake had been drained, leaving a swathe of dead fish, a sad, sorry sight. But nature was fighting back and pumps worked frantically to hold back the water which kept seeping back from underground. I cursed the pumps and prayed for more flooding!

Tensions were mounting in the village. People were taking sides. I felt the hostility of many. The mayor no longer spoke to me and the developers gave me dirty looks. My health began to suffer. I slept badly and hardly at all when the police took away my passport and the local council put a ban on work continuing at my house. The passport episode was particularly upsetting, for it was summarily demanded of me one day when I was sitting in Abidin's office and despite his intervention, the soldier sent to get it insisted I must give it. No reason was given as to why they wanted it. That's what bothered me. I was living then in Turkey with a tourist visa valid for three months and my visa was within the time-limit. I gave my passport, but only after Abidin had telephoned our friend the governor and been assured I would get it back that day.

I got my passport back. Ten lays later the ban on building at my house was lifted . . . with no explanation.

Günther had invited me to visit him in Germany. He wanted me to sing at a fund-raising event he was organising. It was a perfect escape from the pressures for a short while and I took it.

I had written my song 'Star of Dalyan', but had no arrangement as yet. Günther suggested my making a record of it with my other song 'Merhaba'. He thought it would be good propaganda for our cause and I agreed. I went to Stuttgart and then to Munich where Günther had organised a recording studio and an arranger for me. Mats Björlund the owner of the studio and a brilliant musician charged nothing for the use of the studio. He was a sympathiser. I was deeply grateful for his help and for the wonderful recording he made. The record, a 45 rpm. had 'Star of Dalyan' on one side and, on the other, another song I had written on the journey to Stuttgart – 'Iztuzu Blues'. It was a protest song, but not a heavy one, it had a fast beat. I financed the actual pressing of the records and the art work. The sleeve showed an aerial view of our beach on one side; on the other Günther's AGA logo of a turtle and a photo of me. A notice said that 'part of the proceeds of the sale of this record would be given to turtle protection'.

We hoped to promote our cause through the record and Günther arranged for it to be played on German radio.

I returned to Dalyan refreshed and ready for whatever the rest of the summer had in store.

Chapter Thirteen

Haydibay the Bear

I hadn't been back in Dalyan long when rumours began to make the rounds that I was a spy! This incredible claim made me laugh until I realised that some people believed it.

An article had appeared in a Turkish daily in which I had been described as a *Greek* spy. It was said that I was trying to undermine Turkish tourism with my conservation activities. I was reported as being a frequent traveller to Greece. In fact, that was true, I did go from Marmaris to Rhodes on occasion to renew my three-month visa. I also had been to Athens that year. But the most damning bit of 'evidence' against me was that I had made a present of a T-shirt illustrated with a turtle, and this T-shirt bore the label – Made in Greece. Reading this I laughed myself silly and thought of a bawdy retort to the newspaper reporter should I ever meet him – 'My underwear says Paris, but that doesn't make me a French tart.'

It was all so pathetic and naïve. I had had 20 T-shirts made in Greece by an English girlfriend who had drawn me a wonderful design of a turtle on a beach; these T-shirts were for my own use and/or to be given to friends. One of the Kavala architects had begged me for one and, in the interests of harmony between us, I had given it.

The story of my being a Greek spy persisted for a while, but died a natural death in time. Perhaps someone did take it seriously though, for I had two unusual encounters in Dalyan during the summer. One was a stranger who tried to pick me up in a shop, speaking first English, then Greek. I suspected his over-friendly manner and his curiosity about me and left him standing. I never set eyes on him again. The second encounter was with a Turkish man who phoned me at Abidin's office on several occasions saying he was a Green and wanted to help with the turtles. One day he arrived in Dalyan with a young lady whom he

84

introduced as his wife. Both spoke impeccable English, but they had a strange story to tell. He said he was an officer in the Turkish army and must stay in the army until he was middle-aged; this he did not want to do, he wanted to get out of the army now. If he could marry a foreign woman, he would automatically be released. I listened in astonishment to this.

The officer class of the military are the elite of the country and this tale simply did not seem plausible and why were they telling me? The answer soon came.

'You are foreign and unmarried. We could marry,' said the young man.

'But you are married,' I said, indicating his young wife.

'We would divorce. You and I would marry and after three months we would divorce and then I'd remarry my wife.'

I gaped at them. I was angry. Why did they think they could involve me in such a shifty business? I told them so, adding that he was privileged to be an officer in the Turkish army and should do his duty.

They went off not looking too pleased. I never saw them or heard from them again.

Abidin was intrigued when I recounted the story to him.

'They were probably Secret Police. Do you realise how serious it is to be involved in subversion against the army? Perhaps they carried a tape recorder. What did you say? You could be in trouble.'

I said, 'They did talk about politics too, but I told them I have no political allegiances.'

'There are many informers in my country,' said Abidin. 'Be careful, maybe someone wishes you harm. Remember the passport?'

I told him about the other man, the one in she shop who had tried to pump me to get me to speak Greek.

'How stupid people can be, you only want to help my country. I want to help too. I want my sons to grow up with clean air, clean minds, the way I did.' Abidin threw back his head looking like his old, Lionself . . . he had no sons as yet . . . nor even a wife . . .

'Be careful,' he said, 'even about getting married.' There was no fear of that. I had no desire to jump out of the frying pan into the fire.

I knew about intrigue, innuendo and gossip from my exposure to the Old Man; they were much-used weapons around here, so when a group of young people arrived from Izmir saying they intended to form a Turkish Green Party and would I be their leader, said a firm 'No'. They went down to Iztuzu beach and stayed there three days on a hunger strike. This too attracted the press.

I went to visit them, however, and found Professor Erdal there. We had a long talk and I learned that he too was having problems in Dalyan, this from local men who resented his lecturing them on saving their village from unsuitable development. He had taken a series of photographs showing the contrast between attractive old buildings, beautiful scenery and the ugly, concrete, Lego-style buildings now going up. Criticism of any sort was not welcome in the village and he too was getting the cold-shoulder treatment. I could sense the conflict and frustration in this educated, aware man and understood more clearly why Friends of Dalyan had never got off the ground.

At home something completely different had my attention. I had acquired a bear cub. He was an orphan, about seven months old. I had found him while on a visit to my old friend, Aşik Kaptan (Love Kaptan) who lived in a remote village on the coast beyond Marmaris. I went there, with Ibrahim, for the wedding of the *kaptan*'s son. Two days of feasting end dancing, during which time I was shown the bear cub. He was kept in appalling conditions, on a piece of bare earth with no shade, no water, no food. Though I knew nothing about bears, I could tell he was in distress, for he paced back and forth incessantly, moaning. Questions put to his 'owner' elicited the information that the cub's mother had been shot at a place way up in the mountains on the Datcha peninsula; he had eventually been bought by his present 'owner' who would teach him to dance and earn money from entertaining the tourists.

I consulted Ibrahim and we decided to take the bear home with us if his owner would sell him. Ibrahim undertook the negotiations and a price was finally agreed. In fact, bears are 'protected' in Turkey and the buying and selling of them dubious, but I could not leave the poor creature to such a dismal future and even though my garden was not the perfect place for a wild animal, I knew he would be cared for and loved by us. Ibrahim was able to use the illegal aspects of the adoption to our advantage by scaring the man with risk of exposure. We acquired the bear for the equivalent of about £25. The village carpenter made a travelling cage for him and we set off back to Dalyan, first by boat, then in the ancient Willys jeep I had bought some months before.

We presented a bizarre picture as we had also offered a lift to a German couple, also guests of Aşik Kaptan; they were on their way to

86

the airport after holidaying in Turkey and laden down with Louis Vuitton luggage. Ibrahim drove the old jeep, looking like a bear himself; the bear's cage surmounted all the luggage; I sat next to Ibrahim with the strong scent of bear in my nostrils and the two Germans were squeezed in the back – all open and exposed to wind and dust for we had no roof.

Ibrahim had no driving licence, but would not let me drive; the jeep had a road licence, but no insurance; there was no handbrake and no windscreen wipers; these omissions, together with our bizarre appearance end the presence of a 'protected' bear on board would surely have got us stopped by police in any other country, but Turkey has a laissez-faire attitude in many respects and we got back without being arrested.

The bear was called Alibay, or Mr Ali, but we changed it to Haydibay, Mr Haydi, this because the mayor of Dalyan village was named Mr Ali and we did not wish to give offence by having an animal of the same name.

Haydibay was tethered to a long rope in the garden and used his travelling crate as a sleeping den. We stuffed him with food to compensate for his months of malnutrition; he ate everything we offered, from yoghourt to fruit, bread, fish, salad, eggs. As I had earlier sought information about turtles, I now set about finding out about the needs of bears. I wrote to Bern in Switzerland where I had a friend and she put me in touch with the head of the Bear Park there – Professor Sägesser. Soon we were writing and phoning each other.

I loved my garden and home, a green oasis, a refuge from the heat, dust, noise and ever-growing ugliness of the village. The mayor considered concrete synonymous with progress and was handing out building permits like confetti to anyone who would tear down an old house, cut trees or blight a new piece of land. I had some time previously endowed him with a distinguishing nickname as was wont in the village – we had Taxi Ali, Wine Ali and Ali Corn – the mayor became Beton Ali (Concrete Ali).

It stuck, and today, Ali Gün is still privately known as Concrete Ali. As time went on, the mayor became internationally known and was reported in at least one German newspaper as Beton Ali. He was the representative not only of the village, but of his country, as more and more protocol arrived from abroad and from government offices in Ankara. A notable arrival that summer was Karitas Hensel, German Green Party parliamentarian. She was a dynamic campaigner for Green issues and soon became a regular visitor to the village. She was graciously received by Beton Ali and set about, as she herself put it to me, 'educating him politically'. Familiar as I was with the local macho scene, I did not foresee her succeeding but, serene in her Northern European Woman's Lib cocoon, she battled on, sitting for hours in Beton Ali's office and eating copious luncheons and dinners with him and members of the municipality and other experts and VIPs. A petite, mid-thirties lady of considerable enthusiasm and charm, she struck a great blow for nature protection and at the same time for a melding of the old-style villagers and the ever-increasing foreign newcomers. We were frequently together and, on one of her visits, insisted on handing me a donation for Friends of Dalyan, for she too hoped it would be founded. In the event, I had a batch of T-shirts made with the money and these were sold by Nergis's group in Istanbul and Günther's in Germany. This time the T-shirts were 'Made in Turkey'.

A two-man team came from Turkish television TRT. I knew them from my visit to their offices in Ankara. They asked me to be their guide and I took them on the usual tour of the delta, this time including the ancient ruined city of Caunos, which lies within half a mile of Dalyan. There they shot some marvellous footage, for Caunos stands on a rock (the Lion Rock) commanding stupendous views of delta, beach and Dalyan. Uğur and Mehmet were half my age and climbing to the summit of the Lion Rock carrying their filming equipment posed no problem. I staggered behind them panting and pausing and finally made it to the top to be rewarded with a breathtaking view of my 'paradise'. All the ugliness of concrete, vehicles, neon signs, electricity grids and power lines were as though smudged out and one saw only the glistening river linking lake and beach; the slender minaret of the mosque aligned with the many poplars; the majesty of the cliffs; the dark covering of the forests and the little red-roofed houses lying snugly below.

At dinner one night at the Denizati *restoran*, Uğur end Mehmet heard me sing my song '*Merhaba*' and liked it so much they asked me to record it on film. Next day, they filmed me on a boat on the river, singing my song. It was impromptu, I had no proper makeup and was wearing my usual simple village gear of knee-length pants and T-shirt (turtle one of course), but we had fun and the resulting ten-minute film was shown on Turkish television several times that summer.

The song itself, just the sound-track, was subsequently used many times as background music to a series of promotion clips on TV put out by the Ministry of Tourism. The irony appealed to me for I was aware of the continued friction existing between that ministry and conservationists.

More tourists came to Dalyan that summer. Many were attracted by the publicity, and especially by the turtles; they had come there to 'see them'. We conservationists redoubled our efforts to get the beach declared 'out of bounds' at night. Nergis, Günther, Keith, Karitas, Dr Gurpinar, NGOs and many others pressured in various ways to this end.

A team of 'experts' was sent from Ankara to assess the situation; they came on one of the hottest days in September and were escorted down to the beach in two boats by the mayor and his supporters. All wore suits, ties, and of course, shoes. The ladies from Ankara, of whom there were several – town planners, biologists, bureaucrats – were dressed hotly and chastely in two-piece suits and wore high-heeled shoes. It was chaos on the beach, trying to land them in their unsuitable clothes and footwear ... they could not take off their shoes for they were wearing stockings and, as a result, all had to be trans-shipped and taken out by sea to the other end of the beach at Iztuzu to view the famous beach and the hotel building. The sea journey took half and hour, there were waves and some of the experts looked green by the time we arrived at the tiny, rickety landing stage at Iztuzu. The boatmen had to carry the ladies ashore, while the men removed shoes and socks, hitched up their trouser legs and waded ashore. The ladies then staggered across the hot sand to the building site some hundred yards away.

Nergis and I, wearing shorts and being barefoot had no problems. We also had our bathing suits underneath and while the others sweated and stumbled around the site, she and I went for a swim in the sea.

An al fresco picnic was then served in the dilapidated remains of a former beach *bufé* (buffet), on a small cliff at the extreme end of the beach. A message had been sent to Dalyan and a couple of minibuses now came to pick up the sufferers and take them back to the village.

Eyeing them staggering to the bus, Nergis said to me, 'What are they doing here, deciding the fate of the turtles, of this place? They have no idea about nature.' I agreed with her. Indeed, what hope had we got?

Abidin found me a couple of days later and told me that he had heard that Nergis and I had caused a scandal on the beach by exposing our bodies and swimming in view of the experts. I was incredulous! He looked stern, 'They say you were provoking the men by showing your bodies.'

'People do swim on beaches,' I said. 'And anyway they were

supposed to be looking at the building site, not us.' He grinned, 'This is Turkey,' he said.

Something new had appeared on the beach that summer – topless women! I wondered how this would equate with Turkish morals and dreams of tourist expansion. Sun umbrellas had also made their first appearance on our beach. They looked unsightly with their bright colours and Coca-Cola, Tuborg Beer advertisements, but worse than that, they were a menace to the turtles' nests. We now knew from turtle experts that a change in the temperature of the sand could prevent the eggs hatching or influence the sex ratio of the hatchlings. A slightly lower temperature and only males would hatch from a nest – the shade of a beach umbrella over a period of hours could cause this.

We redoubled our efforts to get some ordinances made for protection of the beach and to have signs put up, informing the public about the turtles and asking their co-operation. We also continued in our efforts to get some rubbish bins put on the beach. As the number of visitors increased, so did the litter, on the beach, in the river and in the village. Motor vehicles still drove along the beach occasionally. We were desperate for help from the authorities in Ankara but official matters move slowly and we had to wait. The future of Dalyan and of the flora and fauna was being decided in Ankara.

When the summer was almost over, we got good news. The signs were to be erected on the beach: NO MOTOR VEHICLES. NO NIGHT-TIME VISITS. NO DIGGING OF HOLES. NO UMBRELLA WITHIN 30 METRES OF THE SEA. We were ecstatic about the signs, but they came too late to help that year.

At the end of October conservation in Dalyan received a superb boost. David Bellamy, the famous TV personality and conservation crusader, came to the village with several members of the British press. I was thrilled, not only for our cause, but personally, for I had long admired him and hoped that one day I might meet him and ask his help.

Now my dream was reality and I sat at dinner in the Denizati *restoran*, by the river, next to the great man himself. I found him to be as charismatic as on his TV appearances. He was also very warm and humorous. The journalists with him represented the *Observer* and *The Times*. BBC Radio 2 was also represented. I spent three event-packed days with them, escorted them about the delta, sang them my songs, invited them to my house. David was especially delighted to meet Haydibay, the bear.

Nergis had arranged a fund-raising dinner in Istanbul at which David

Bellamy was to be guest of honour. Through the kindness of Patricia Daunt, wife of the then British Ambassador to Turkey, Timothy Daunt (now Sir Timothy), Nergis and her group DHKD were able to use the magnificent facilities of the British Consulate in Pera, Istanbul, for the dinner.

The British Consulate, formerly the embassy in Ottoman times, is a vast and beautiful eighteenth-century palace standing in a glorious park in the centre of Istanbul.

The dinner, attended by three hundred guests, was a glittering affair; the first major fund-raising on behalf of conservation to take place in Turkey.

David Bellamy, as guest of honour, made a fine speech after dinner. The guests were mostly Turkish, professional people, industrialists, the socially prominent and many were members of Nergis's DHKD organisation.

I had been asked to sing my songs following David's speech. He introduced me and I heard the strains of my song 'Iztuzu Blues' coming from the stereo system. I sang, putting all my emotion into the performance, the image of the beach in my mind. I carried the microphone and walked from table to table singing to these special people, all of whom were there tonight because they supported the idea of environmental protection. It was a highlight for me, as a musician and as a conservationist. The audience applauded my first song and I began to sing the romantic 'Star of Dalyan', evocative of the Dalyan river and the moonlight which inspired me to write it. My dress, of white chiffon embroidered with silver beads, glittered in the light of the room's great chandeliers.

The last notes faded and I took my bow – it wasn't easy for my eyes were full of tears.

Chapter Fourteen

Acceptance

All in all 1987 had been a positive year for the campaign in Dalyan. We were still not out of the wood but powerful forces were at work on our side and Nergis's DHKD gala evening in Istanbul, attended by many of Turkey's elite, proved by its success that environmental issues were gaining importance in the country.

One more event of huge implications took place before the end of that year – the Turkish government announced that the size of the Holiday Village complex at Iztuzu was to be reduced from 1,800 beds to 600.

All the campaigners were elated, though we could have wished for no beds at all but it was great news and, not easily satisfied, we hoped for better in 1988.

The reason for the government's decision had to do with an environmental impact study that had been carried out on the beach by two German environmental experts, Dr Kinselbach and Dr Schemmel. Credit must be given to the Kavala group who commissioned this study. It should, of course, have been done by the Turkish authorities *before* building permission was granted ... but it wasn't.

I knew the two experts and had had frequent conversations with them. The results of their study were circulated amongst those involved in the turtle campaign; their recommendations were as follows: first and best solution no beds; second solution 600 beds; third (advise against) 1,800 beds.

The Turkish government had compromised and taken the middle path. It was a commendable decision and a brave one in the, then, atmosphere of tourist expansion, foreign investment, development and profit.

Some years later I met Dr Schemmel again in Dalyan and was

overjoyed when he told me that he and Dr Kinselbach had used my 1985 Proposal for the Establishment of a National Park, Dalyan Delta, as a guideline for their early studies. Coming from these informed men, it was a compliment I cherished.

The winter of 1987–8 I stayed in Europe. Ibrahim had built himself a small house in my garden and looked after my animals during my absence.

Articles about Dalyan continued to appear in the press in Turkey and abroad; the *Frankfürter Algemeine*, *Le Monde*, the *Wall Street Journal* and *Der Spiegel* were amongst these. Several excellent pieces were written by the journalists who had accompanied David Bellamy to Dalyan. I was asked to broadcast an update on BBC Radio 2. I spoke about the turtles and, on a separate occasion, about Haydibay the bear.

Many organisations, governmental and non-governmental, were active in 1987–8 on behalf of Dalyan; individuals too continued in their efforts. Extremely important help was also given by visits from eminent biologists. Max Kasparek, a noted biologist and expert on Turkish wildlife, was a frequent visitor, highly experienced in fieldwork, not only at Dalyan but in other areas of Turkey. Bryan Groombridge; an eminent herpatologist, from Great Britain, also provided important data. The WWF sent Clare Whitmore who, in collaboration with DHKD, did useful scientific work. Hydrologists came to study the water quality and geomorphologists to write reports about the beach, reed beds and erosion. Others followed, including Riccardo Jesu, a young herpatologist from Italy. One cannot overestimate the importance of the part played by these experts in the Dalyan story.

That winter, I met Lily and Keith in London, both very active – she with her Hellenic Society for the Protection of Nature, he at the Council of Europe. In Istanbul on my way home that spring I stayed with Nergis. DHKD was growing rapidly in importance and in the numbers of its members.

So I returned to Dalyan in March 1988 in high hopes and delighted to be back in my own home, to be welcomed by the animals and to enjoy the garden now green and bursting with life.

Haydibay had grown enormously and was now up to my shoulder. Ibrahim and he enjoyed a friendly if boisterous relationship and would wrestle each day for an hour or so amongst the lemon, fig and orange trees in the garden. For this encounter, Ibrahim always wore an old ski jacket and long trousers for the bear's teeth and claws were formidable. He was not an aggressive creature but could unintentionally have caused serious hurt. The rest of the day he was tethered on a long chain amongst the trees and would shin up his favourites with the speed and agility of an ape. He also ate whatever fruit there was (except citrus) and destroyed bark and branches. Every few days he was moved to a new area so as to give the trees and grass a chance to recover. He loved water and spent a fair amount of time in the small stream running through the property. As the days grew hotter, Ibrahim gave him a daily shower with the garden hose. This he loved. At night Haydibay was put in the large cage we had had built for him. He usually slept on his back, paws in the air, in his den which was like a cave. Each morning I brought him his breakfast of milk, bread, fruit and honey. He knew my voice and would amble to the bars and survey me with his small eyes as he awaited his dish. Alas, he had a passion for live chickens and killed a few that stupidly eased their way into his cage – not a feather was left.

But Haydibay's future concerned me. He wasn't only a danger to chickens, but as he grew bigger could become one to humans. I knew that I had to confront this problem in the not-too-distant future.

Professor Sägesser of Dälholtzli Zoo in Bern wanted to have him there for a breeding programme that the Swiss government was backing. All the bears at present in the zoo, with one exception, a female, had been born in captivity. Haydibay, as a strong example of his species, born in the wild, was highly desirable as a stud. The possibilities we had looked at of keeping him in Turkey were poor.

'Return him to the wild,' Nergis said, after visiting him.

I knew it would mean certain death for him. Bears born in the wild spend two years with their mothers before being able to fend for themselves. Haydibay had had no such education. Also, he was used to humans and would have undoubtedly approached them, looking for food. One could imagine the panic that would ensue and the subsequent shooting of him. As to giving him to a Turkish zoo, the climate would have been too hot in summer. Bears live in the mountains at high altitude and suffer in the heat. Dalyan was no more suitable – I had seen that. Bern seemed to be the best.

Professor Sägesser and I continued to exchange letters and phone calls. Telephone connections had improved slightly in Dalyan and though I still did not have a phone in my home, my name was on a waiting list and I used the post office.

If Haydibay's future was uncertain, so was mine. The atmosphere in the village was still not good – people took sides and many wanted the hotel. I was still cold-shouldered by some. Then something occurred to

94

make me acceptable. *Guneş*, a Turkish daily newspaper, printed an article about me on its front page, saying that I had been responsible for an economic boom in Dalyan due to my care for the turtles. Dalyan had become famous wrote the journalist; more and more tourists were coming and artefacts of all kinds, representing turtles, were being snapped up in the shops. A photo of me accompanied the story.

Before long, people were smiling at me once more and in due course, Kuno and Lily greeted me. I was glad for our friendship was dear to me and I had missed their company.

A contributing factor to the thaw was that Nergis, had had news-sheets printed with an analysis of the economic advantages to be expected from the Iztuzu Hotel complex: it was negative, most of the profit would remain in Germany; the hotel would have its own shops, transport and the hotel staff would be mostly imported from Germany or other parts of Turkey. All in all, not much money would accrue to Dalyan village. The hotel complex would also be out-of-bounds to non-residents and therefore not much use in a new and popular local pastime – making contact with the tourists.

Suddenly I began to get requests for turtle T-shirts and stickers. I gave away a few T-shirts and lots of stickers, logos from DHKD and AGA. Soon they were plastered around the village and no self-respecting taxi-driver or minibus owner would be seen without one or more adorning his vehicle.

This was a signal for the renaming of old businesses and new ones and a spate of *Caretta caretta*, Turtle, and Natur (Nature) broke out.

Dalyan was growing in leaps with more buildings, of the Lego variety, going up everywhere. Ali Gün, the mayor had, the year before, given the first licence for a three-storey building in the village. This was the Kaunos Hotel, owned by the municipality. It was an unfortunate decision, for the building's height destroyed the natural balance of the landscape and obscured the marvellous view of the cliffs on the other side of the river. Worse still, it was a forerunner to a plethora of other three-storey buildings being constructed. But the mayor was within his rights for, some months earlier, the PTT had begun work on a new post office at the entrance to Dalyan's main street and this was growing upwards like Jack's beanstalk and now towered five storeys high, its height and size dwarfing all around it. A great deal of criticism had been expressed against this monster, not only by locals, who liked their old post office, but by visitors who deplored the change in village style and especially by the German Greens, who objected to it for a variety of reasons. In her discussions with the mayor, Karitas Hensel had promised to secure for Dalyan a large amount of Deutsch marks as compensation in the event the hotel should not be built. The Greens now negotiated with the PTT officials in Ankara for the *demolition* of the building! This did not work but they did succeed in influencing this government-controlled agency to knock off the two top storeys. Some extremely critical investigative reporting, which appeared in the Turkish press, was also responsible for this extraordinary decision. News was leaked that the two top floors of the 'skyscraper' were in fact intended as luxury holiday homes for the upper echelons of the PTT management. Demolition began in 1989. Throughout the spring and early summer of that year, the village pulsated to the sounds of sledgehammers and pneumatic drills, while the clouds of dust arising from the resulting ruins enveloped all as though in a *hamsin* in the desert. I inhaled the dust and bent my ear to the scream of the drills appreciatively . . . for once air and noise pollution were not offensive.

A journalist friend came to do a story and expressed his dismay at the changes evident in the village since his last visit.

'What's that?' he asked, gesturing towards the PTT disaster.

'The new PTT building, but they're knocking off the two top storeys, thank God!'

'The entire place is a mess,' he said.

We walked to a quieter place, a café overlooking the Lycian tombs and ordered drinks. I gazed at these splendid rock tombs as they glowed ochre-pink in the sun's low rays, remembering my first sight of them all those years before.

'I suppose they'll be floodlighting those before long,' he said, looking at the tombs.

'Oh! yes. The mayor has plans, he wants them floodlit blue,' I told him.

My friend shuddered and said contemptuously, 'Concrete everywhere. Those awful sun-energy installations on the roofs. Buildings like bunkers . . . next thing there'll be discos.'

'We've got one of those already,' I said.

'Well, they're ruining this beautiful place.'

Indeed he was right. Dalyan village was becoming an ugly, commercial blot on the landscape. I was glad my own home was outside town a bit and still a peaceful haven.

A television crew came from BBC 2. They were making a David Bellamy Nature programme. In my garden they interviewed me and

96

filmed the hut, the dogs and Haydibay shinning up a palm tree. The film was shown later that summer in the UK.

The house now finished, I began to look around for a boat. Ibrahim found a suitable, not-new one and we began negotiations to buy it. Not easy, for it appeared to have a number of owners and to rocket in price with the emergence of each.

Avoiding many pitfalls and tricks, we finally acquired the boat, a 23-foot rivercraft with one mast and a cabin. Like the hut, she was modest and endearing. I christened her *Star of Dalyan* and we took her to the boatyard where Ibrahim set about painting and varnishing her. Soon she was back in the water and I could assume the rank of *kaptan* again.

Now I could go to the beach whenever I wanted and even sleep there, for there was a cabin and I could stay on board and not break the ban on visiting the beach at night. Mr Sandy, then my oldest dog, proved himself a keen sailor and rarely missed a boat trip with me. In the early mornings, I walked the sand once more, looking for tracks and floated on the satiny sea reliving my old days of beach life, while Sandy kept a lookout to ensure I wasn't carried off to Rhodes.

One night there was a happy reunion with some old beach-dwellers in Dalyan village. Yildirim (Lightning), now some twelve years old, had his circumcision party. This is an important event in the life of a Muslim male, perhaps the most important. I had been to other such celebrations, but was particularly proud when Yildirim, dressed in white pants and red satin cloak, with a white satin hat embroidered with tinsel, invited me on to the floor for the first dance. He looked like a boy-prince. Mother and father, Tayfun, (Typhoon) looked on happily. It was a memorable evening of feasting end dancing but I left before midnight, when I saw our village doctor arrive to cut the boy.

In the next weeks Professor Sägesser and I continued to correspond about Haydibay. It was a sad time for me, because, although I was making the arrangements for him to go, I did not want him to leave. Each day I grew fonder of him and dreaded the day he must go. In the meantime, he made his own attempts to see the outside world, once escaping into the cotton fields adjoining the house and munching happily on the buds. This was a disaster, for cotton is an important crop and I had to pay damages. Fortunately, he wasn't free for long.

The next escape was worse, as Ibrahim was away visiting his village. A young Italian herpatologist, Riccardo Jesu, helping out with a study on turtles, was staying in the hut.

'Riccardo!' I yelled, when there was no sign of Haydibay.

We found him eventually in the neighbour's garden, up a tree eating plums. Nearby, an apprehensive crowd of local women and children watched. A length of chain hung from the bear's neck. With considerable courage, Riccardo managed to get near enough to attach the chain to a rope, which he then tethered to the foot of the tree. At least Haydibay could not leave there, but how to get him back home? We couldn't. In the end he was still there at nightfall and we went to bed in trepidation in case he should free himself.

The next morning, to my relief, Haydibay was back in his cage waiting for breakfast.

It seems Ibrahim had returned late at night and when he saw that the bear wasn't in his cage, nor in the garden, he made some special bear sounds, known only to him and Haydibay. From the next door garden came answering sounds and Ibrahim climbed the fence and brought his friend back.

It was irresponsible to delay any longer – Haydibay had to be sent away. All was arranged. Swissair had most kindly offered to pay the bear's transport expenses and a free ticket for me to accompany him. All seemed ready. We set a date. Then another of those bureaucratic absurdities stymied all our plans – the ministry of Forestry (custodians of wildlife) refused an export permit for Haydibay.

I was leaving for England for a week, to attend the wedding of friends, so had to abandon everything until my return. It was the beginning of June and getting hot. Haydibay spent most of his days lying in the little stream, trying to cool off.

On the eve of my departure, Turgut Özal made a surprise visit to Dalyan. It was his first and I found the village in a spin as I parked my bicycle outside the old post office. Flags were everywhere, some foreign, mostly Turkish. A dais had been erected on the square near the river and waiters bustled putting out tables and chairs. The mayor and some of his sidekicks hovered about in city clothes, looking hot.

There was lots of security, *jandarma* and police. Crowds began to gather and I saw Abidin's lionhead above the throng on the outskirts and barged my way towards him.

Suddenly police and officials cleared a path and Turgut Özal's sturdy frame came into view. His wife, the governor and other dignitaries followed and soon all were seated at the top table. The lesser fry stood around. I managed to reach Abidin.

The village band had now burst forth in ragged cacophony playing the national anthem. We all stood to attention.

Bright sunlight and swallows dipping and swooping from river to eucalyptus trees. A few stray dogs loped warily on the quay. Men stood on their boats watching the scene.

Mr Özal spoke. His voice blared from a series of microphones installed around the square. I caught some words, particularly the ones about a Mili Park – National Park. Was my dream, begun in 1984, about to come true? I turned to Abidin. 'What did he say?'

'He says Dalyan has been declared an SPA – Specially Protected Area, something better than a National Park.'

I was thrilled and told him so. More speeches and then the assembly broke up and the guards formed a path to let the prime minister through to his waiting limousine. Abidin grabbed my hand.

'Come on,' he said, 'you're going to meet the prime minister.'

We reached the car just as the Özals were ready to get in. The mayor and a couple of councillors stood by looking pleased with themselves.

'Excuse me, sir,' said Abidin to Mr Özal, holding out his hand to be shaken. 'I am Abidin Kurt of this village.' Mr Özal looked up at him and took his hand, greeting him.

Abidin indicated me. 'May I introduce this lady. She is the turtle lady of Dalyan.'

Turgut Özal shook hands with me.

'How do you do?' he said in English, 'thank you, we need people like you.'

He and Mrs Özal moved towards the car. Just before getting in he turned in our direction and said, 'Remember, we need you.'

I stood there stunned. Whether he meant me personally or conservationists in general, it was good to hear it. They drove away. Abidin and I looked at each other, beaming. I was glad that the mayor had witnessed this. Perhaps he would speak to me now.

Chapter Fifteen

Turtle Triumph

Two days later I was in London when Keith Corbett delivered some momentous news – the Turkish government had *cancelled* the hotel project at Iztuzu. Later Günther phoned me to tell me the same thing.

'Much is due to you,' I said. 'Congratulations.'

'And congratulations to you, Kaptan June.'

No hotel. It was fabulous news. I called Lily, Nergis, Karitas – all links in the chain of victory.

A few days later I was to return to Dalyan. In those days I visited the offices of The Conservation Foundation, and met their director, David Shreeve. David Bellamy had arranged this. David Shreeve received me warmly and we talked of Dalyan and the recent developments. I told him I had sought funding from AGA and DKHD for a new batch of T-shirts I wanted to have made, but that both had said they could not help. A couple of days later he called me to say that the foundation would fund the T-shirts.

And so I returned to Dalyan well pleased with the results of my stay there.

I travelled via Istanbul and was to stay at Nergis's home; when I got there I found she was away and her sister Mevce put me up for one night. I was surprised not to find Nergis as we had spoken just a few days before and she had said nothing of leaving.

She had left me a note which said she had had to go to Adana on urgent business. Mevce said, 'Nergis will be in Dalyan tomorrow night for the turtle victory celebrations.'

I was astonished and queried, 'Celebrations . . . turtle celebrations . . . who's organised it?'

'I don't know,' said Mevce, 'but I think it's got something to do with the Germans.'

Indeed I found the news surprising for I had spoken to all of my collaborators in the past week and had heard nothing about it.

I did not sleep well, waking at odd hours, excited by the thought of the turtle celebrations and wondering why I had not been told.

Next day I flew to Dalaman airport, from whence by *taksi* to Dalyan. I found all well at home, though Ibrahim was in a gloomy mood. He had been given to moodiness in the past weeks and I suspected it had to do with the departure of Haydibay. Ibrahim did not want him to go.

'He is worth a fortune,' he told me, 'you cannot just give him away like that.'

I had never thought of Haydibay in terms of money or profit, in fact, he had cost me quite a bit with his voracious appetite and the expense of building his cage, not to mention damages paid for his foray into the cotton field.

'You should sell him,' said Ibrahim, sitting crosslegged on the floor of my, kitchen sipping his glass of tea.

I was appalled and dismissed the idea out-of-hand.

'I could teach him to dance and he could earn money from the tourists or we could wrestle like we do here. They would love it. We could take him down to the beach – there are so many people in summer – we could make a fortune.' I was even more appalled. I had thought Ibrahim to be 'different', more enlightened, but now saw how wrong I was. When he saw there was no way of changing my mind, he loped off to his little house in a huff, looking like a bear himself.

I went to the village to find out about the turtle celebrations. After a while I found Günther at the Denizati *restoran*. It was true, the party was tonight at the other Denizati *restoran* (there were now two, one on either end of the quay) and it had been organised between the German Greens and Ankara. VIPs were coming from Ankara, including the minister for Labour and Welfare, a woman, Imren Aykut.

I had sung the year before at the opening of Denizati Two *restoran*. Now Günther asked me if I would sing that evening. I hesitated, for I wasn't too sure about this whole turtle jamboree, which seemed to me to be premature and something akin to crowing, not a good thing in view of the considerable opposition the village had shown to environmental protection. But I am fond of Günther and said yes. He rushed off nervous and sweating to the Denizati Two. Watching him go I thought how much he had changed in the short time since he had first come to Dalyan; he had been mellower then, fitter ... now he looked like any city man under stress.

I went to the *restoran* a little earlier that evening as I wanted to check my musical backup. The band had arrived and were setting up their microphones and instruments. Nergis was there looking even more stressed than Günther and a German Master of Ceremonies, in charge of all, handled his task like a circus-master. I knew him. We had met on the beach years before and he had wanted to found Friends of Dalyan with Erdal and me. I hadn't heard of him for years. What was he doing here and in charge? He greeted me effusively and said that I should give my performance immediately after the speeches. Speeches! I was dismayed … I knew Turkish evenings involving VIPs from Ankara who made speeches … they were long and boring.

It was a glorious evening with an almost full moon and a magical spread of stars. The river shone with reflected lights and candles on the tables flamed softly. The perfume of night-scented flowers was on the air. Glasses tinkled as waiters set the tables and there was the slap-slap of water on hull as boats moored alongside the quay responded to the movement of the river.

The night was warm, but I felt comfortable in a red sleeveless blouse and black silk skirt.

I approached Nergis who was placing cards at the top table. She looked attractive in a smart blue dress. After the usual greetings and inquiries about her little girl, Ayşe, of whom I am very fond, I asked her where I should sit.

'Sit?' she looked at me in a distracted way. 'Sit anywhere you like.' I chose a place somewhere beyond the salt and put my purse there.

'Oh! no, you can't sit here,' she said, 'this is reserved for protocol.' There were at least 20 places at the table. 'Sit at one of the other tables,' she added.

I did not consider myself 'protocol' nor of special importance, but was upset not to be seated with my collaborators. Günther and his wife, Gitte, Nergis and Karitas, all had their names on place cards on the table.

Other guests were arriving and I found a place with some friends. The organiser appeared again.: 'Don't forget, you sing immediately after the speeches.'

Somehow my enthusiasm for singing that evening had waned. The place was filling up. TV teams from Turkey and Germany were there and journalists were milling about. One of the latter came up to me. I thought he was going to ask me about the turtles and Dalyan, but he didn't mention either. He wanted to know about my singing.

The band did not play and I couldn't understand why. Usually Turks love music and their sounds would have livened up the proceedings but, in fact, they were waiting for the minister and her entourage to arrive. In the event, she came quite late and by then we were all hungry and some of us bored.

A scurry near the entrance and at last Imren Aykut appeared, accompanied by the mayor, the governor and a posse of other dark-clad men. Mercifully, the band started up and waiters began to serve dinner.

But before this, Günther had come over to me.

'Why aren't you sitting with us?' he asked.

'Nergis said there was no place for me,' I answered.

'But you must sit with us,' he insisted.

'I'm happy enough here.' I said. He went back to the top table and I saw him speaking to Nergis; after a while he came back.

'Come over,' he said, 'they'll put a place for you.' It was kind of him, but I refused and stayed where I was with my friends.

Nergis was seated next to the minister. I recognised Imren Aykut from her appearances on television and photos in the newspapers. She was the only woman in a position of power in Turkey at that time, capable and dynamic.

After dinner she spoke. I did not understand all but got the gist which was that the Turkish government were concerned about protection of the environment and had named Dalyan accordingly as a Specially Protected Area.

The TV cameras were trained on the protocol table and their strobe lights made the night hotter than ever. Karitas sat next to the mayor with his henchmen on either side of them looking like a row of skittles about to be bowled over. Aeons separated their two cultures and I wondered about Karitas's thoughts. The dark-clad henchmen swigged their raki. I knew them all ... shopkeepers, bar owners, farmers.

The organiser bustled about efficiently, clutching his pad of notes and his microphone – he introduced Karitas, who then spoke. Her speech was very much like Imren Aykut's except that she praised the German government for their actions in 'saving' Dalyan and the turtles.

The rest of the guests, including me, were getting restless and longing for some music and fun, but Günther and Nergis were still to speak.

Nergis's speech was again similar to the other ladies'. She offered deserved praise to the Turkish authorities for the saving of the turtles and included her group DRKD in the accolade.

Günther then spoke, agreeing with the others and giving credit to his group AGA. He also mentioned Lily Veneselos and me.

I was glad we had not been completely ignored. But I wished that more credit had been given to the many individuals who had helped to create this Turtle Triumph Celebration.

At last the speeches were over and the band struck up with wild Turkish rhythms. The organiser signalled to me, 'Are you ready?'

Indeed I was not. I did not feel at all like singing. As it happened I didn't have to ... for at that moment, an enormously fat Turkish woman emerged, wearing belly-dancer's costume; she shimmied on to the floor and began to wiggle and jiggle, tassels flying, fringe flailing, while her finger-bells clinked.

It was such an extraordinary contrast to the staid behaviour of the rest of the evening, that I, for one, remained stunned.

Many looked in mute amazement. Even the 'organiser' did not know what was happening.

The buxom entertainer was warming to her audience and now began to dance on the bar, on to which she had been hoisted by two waiters. There was no stopping her, she went on and on until finally the band got exhausted and stopped playing.

It was the first time a belly-dancer had performed in public in Dalyan, perhaps in private too for all I know. While it is an accepted form of entertainment in tourist places today, it was looked upon in villages then as lascivious and unsuitable.

The organiser now came over asking if I would sing.

'No,' I told him. I did not fancy this atmosphere for my songs.

I left quietly without saying goodnight to anyone and went to sit on the quay where there were few people. I looked up at the glorious sky and thought of the beach now, under the moonlight, I thought of its purity and of the turtles, perhaps nesting at this moment, and I contrasted these things with the events of this evening. What did they have in common? I wondered. As far as I could tell the evening had been the stage for a series of ego trips. Few of the guests knew the feel of sand under bare feet and those who did had become enmeshed in a man-made world of politics and power-play. I feared for the future of Dalyan and its flora and fauna, thinking that they were more likely to be manipulated than protected.

Somewhere along the quay a guitar was being played. I went there. A group of young Turks sat on the pavement playing and singing softly. I sat down with them; they knew me. 'Sing,' they said.

I sang 'Summertime'. Passers by stopped and listened. I sang the John Lennon song, 'Imagine' and other tunes – it was a memorable, magical half-hour.

Then I walked home under the stars and went to sleep in the hut, listening to the sound of the reeds on the roof, the bells tinkling, and dreamed I was back on the sandspit in the days when it belonged to the turtles.

Chapter Sixteen

Pandora's Box

The Turtle Triumph Celebration had left me with an uneasy feeling about the future of conservation in Dalyan. As the months went by in the following year, 1989, I was aware that I had inadvertently opened an approximation of Pandora's Box.

Tourists flocked to Dalyan in increasing numbers, even turning up now out of season, that is to say, not just in the hot, summer months as they had done before. Turks were among them, a new thing, for Dalyan had not been a popular destination like Marmaris or Bodrum. We had become famous through press and TV and at the summit of our fame stood the turtle – *Caretta caretta*. People were intrigued and wanted to see them. Others wanted to profit from them. Entrepreneurs of all kinds began to arrive from other parts of the country and some from abroad. Building sites proliferated; new shops and offices opened every day; the municipality was quick to catch on and built on every bit of land in their possession – usually prime land, near the river and in the main street. Soon we had not one carpet shop, but six.

The locals began to jump on the bandwagon, of course, and people who had formerly earned their living as fishermen, farmers, barbers, hauliers, changed jobs to anything connected with tourism. *Pansiyons* were built, houses were enlarged to provide rental accommodation; farmers drove minibuses; barbers opened *restorans* and shops; fishermen didn't fish any more, it was easier and more lucrative to ferry trippers to the beach or Caunos; young men came from the countryside, eager to get rich and to make contact with the tourists, whose fame had also spread via the newspapers. For example, EIGHTY THOUSAND GERMAN WOMEN VISITORS SLEPT WITH TURKISH MEN LAST YEAR was one notable headline which had a dramatiç effect on a male population where chastity and virginity among their own women is strictly enforced.

The fact that hardly anyone spoke a foreign language and knew nothing of the tastes and needs of tourists, did not deter them from trying their luck. Concrete, bunker-style buildings were the order of the day; orange and lemon groves were destroyed; shady terraces gave way to minuscule, sun-exposed balconies overlooking busy roads; flat roofs, surmounted by the ubiquitous water tanks, were now used as bars, each with its own loud music, causing a racket into the small hours. Plateglass windows began to replace the former village-style ones and wooden furniture in cafés and *restorans* were exchanged for plastic.

I thought of the words of Adnan Kahveci, when he had said, 'We want selective tourism for the Dalyan delta.'

The present tasteless 'development' augured ill for that.

Worse still were the threats to flora and fauna. True we had achieved some laws protecting the beach, but how were these going to be enforced in the face of ever-increasing numbers of people and the polluting services they required? There were now at least three hundred boats plying the river, carrying the tourists back and forth, whereas there had been but fifty two years before. Each spewed a certain amount of exhaust fumes and oil into the atmosphere and water and each contributed to the noise pollution. What of birdlife on river and lake?

Dalyan was not the only place in the world to suffer such a fate when assaulted by a sudden influx of people alien to its surroundings and cultures. In fact, the Turkish press had often referred to Spain as an example of the sort of tourist expansion that would not be allowed in Turkey. But here we were, getting the same and worse. Nothing had been properly planned and Dalyan still had the same primitive installations as before; power and water cuts often occurred; telephone lines were inadequate and collapsed with strong winds; garbage disposal was desultory to say the least, there was no proper drainage and no sewage plant. Yet, building went on apace.

My hopes, and those of others who cared about Dalyan and the turtles, were with the SPA team in Ankara, those appointed since the banning of the hotel project as protectors. Some of the advisory signs on the beach and river had blown down in winter storms. I phoned DHKD asking them to replace them but permission was necessary from

Ankara and this took several months to obtain. In the meantime turtles began to nest and even to hatch.

In midsummer Abidin got married. His bride was Elizabeth Hyers, a charming American girl he had met in Turkey the year before. I was glad for him as I knew that he had long wanted to settle down and start a family. Feasting and dancing went on for two days; drums thumped and clarinets wailed even accompanying us on a trip down the river to the beach on one day. As we sailed along the sandbar, I thought of our old days on it, of our huts and of the turtles and how my life had been changed by all this.

Dalyan was getting ever busier and Abidin and I seldom saw each other. Like many a local he was under stress from his own success, as more and more tourists arrived. But I saw that he still retained something of his old beach self as he rushed about the village barefoot and wearing bathing shorts despite carrying a bulging briefcase like any city gent.

At home I enjoyed many blessings. Billie the cat had had kittens and other strays had joined us, so we now had eight cats. Findik had had more puppies and the dog count stood at five. Haydibay, the bear, grew bigger. I was worrying about him. He had to be sent away from Dalyan and soon, but the ministry of Forestry still stood in our path.

Continued efforts on the part of Professor Sägesser proved fruitless and so I decided to go to Ankara and try to find a way there. It was getting hotter, the bear was suffering from the heat and the danger of his escaping and causing damage or injury to neighbours or property was ever present. We had explained this to the ministry but they showed no interest. About that time, both the Swiss and the Turkish press printed articles about him and his problem: VISA REFUSED TO TURKISH BEAR and HAYDIBAY CANNOT TRAVEL.

Through friends in Ankara help came. Haydibay's case was officially put in the hands of the minister of Labour and Social Services, Imren Aykut, the very lady who had been the guest of honour at the Turtle Triumph evening. Why such a ministry should have been chosen for a bear's welfare escapes me to this day, but the results were fine.

Thanks to the goodwill and energy of this powerful lady, Haydibay's visa at last was granted.

The news came to me via the post office and caused quite a stir in the village for, in the way of villages, word got around swiftly. I still did not have a telephone and a message had been received at the post office from Imren Aykut's office that I should phone her in Ankara. As a result of this I was much greeted and deferred to in the village.

108

The PTT staff were agog when I put through my call. I like them all, they are friends of long standing who have been most helpful to me, sending messages to the beach when I lived there and coping with sorting out my mail which came from the four corners of the earth and carried a variety of addresses. A small crowd also gathered by the phone box to witness this communication with power.

I spoke to Imren's Aykut's private secretary, who told me that all was in order for the bear's departure. He made the final arrangements with Swissair for the journey and an Istanbul transport firm was instructed to send a lorry to Dalyan with Haydibay's travelling cage.

On 11 August the lorry arrived at my house. They came in the late afternoon and I was concerned for I knew that the journey to Istanbul was at least fifteen hours and the flight was due to leave the next day.

There were two men in the lorry and we tried to transfer Haydibay from his enclosure to the travelling cage.

It seemed to be an impossible task. Haydibay was afraid and retreated into the corner of his cage. Ibrahim refused to help and sulked in his house. I called two neighbours but we achieved nothing. Then a minor miracle occurred – David Bellamy appeared at my gate. I knew he was in Dalyan, on holiday with his family, indeed we had seen each other, but this visit was quite by chance.

'What's Haydibay's favourite food?' he asked, when I pointed out our dilemma.

'Raw chicken,' I said.

'Bring one,' said David.

Fortunately, I had one defrosting in the fridge. David placed the chicken in the travelling cage, which was brought to within a few inches of the enclosure door. Ibrahim then deigned to give a hand.

'Everyone else disappear,' said David. We did. I waited on the terrace, listening. My thoughts were sad ones. I hated sending Haydibay away and felt like a traitor. Suddenly I heard a 'clang'. It was the door of his travelling cage closing and Haydibay was inside. With considerable effort the cage was carried to the lorry and put on board.

I passed some chunks of water melon through the bars and gave the men a bag full of food for the rest of his journey.

Haydibay looked at me with eyes that told me I was a traitor and the lorry drove away.

I went back to my place on the terrace and cried. David comforted me, then left to join his family. Ibrahim stayed in his house.

Two days later I flew to Zurich and then Bern for the official handing-over of Haydibay at the Dälholtzli Zoo. It had been agreed that he would given by the Turkish government to the Swiss government. I went along as a surrogate mother.

The Turkish ambassador in Bern, Mr Behic Hazer, made the official presentation to Herr Marc-Roland Peter, member of the Swiss National Council.

Haydibay looked on from his cage, munching on a water melon I had brought him from Turkey. He had taken over the resident bears' large enclosure and they were confined in separate, cramped quarters. Beside these zoo-bred bears, he looked magnificent, big and strong, his fur thick and shiny.

TV cameras were there and reporters. I had difficulty holding back the tears.

I said 'good bye' to my friend with a bar of Swiss chocolate.

That night I watched the scene on television. Next day I flew back to Turkey, vowing never again to take a wild creature into my life.

Ibrahim was never the same again. He sulked, was lazy and became dirty in his person.

A friend in Istanbul sent me a newspaper cutting from some weeks before, in it Ibrahim claimed to be Haydibay's rightful owner and said that I had taken the bear only to make a profit. It stated that Haydibay was worth fifty thousand Swiss francs. Ibrahim was quoted as having said that he had proof of being the bear's owner in the form of a written affidavit from the *jandarma* in Selimiye village where we had found Haydibay.

It was, of course, a pack of lies and I was shocked. I challenged Ibrahim about it, but never did get an explanation. To this day I do not know what his motive was. It caused a deep rift between us and I was not sorry when he walked out after a tiff over a trivial matter some weeks later.

I have only seen him once since, when he turned up in Dalyan village briefly, saying he was married and looking dapper in a pearl-grey suit and hat . . . never had I seen him in such splendour. We spoke for a few minutes when we met by chance in the street. He had worked for me for four years and we had been through many vicissitudes in that time, but our paths separated as though we had been but casual acquaintances.

To me it was another example of the difficulties of East meeting West.

Summer progressed with more and more strange people turning up. Misfits and drop-outs were commonplace and the locals were baffled by

110

them. Their belief was that all foreigners were rich and fitted a pattern, especially as seen on TV in such programmes as *Dallas*. When they came across hippies claiming to be English or German, but so poor they lived on tomatoes and bread and slept rough their illusions were shattered. They also did not like the young enthusiasts of good education who came looking to 'save' the turtles. Many dramas and misunderstandings occurred as a result and fights were common at night when alcohol had been consumed and rivalries exploded over the favours of foreign women. The *jandarma* were kept busy.

I too had a couple more trips to the *jandarma* post, once after I had been insulted horribly in a bar by a young local I had befriended on the beach and again when jewellery was stolen from my house.

But my home was a delight, where I could retreat from the ugliness outside. I changed the locks, was more cautious about whom I invited in and engaged a local couple to live in Ibrahim's house as caretakers.

While tourists and locals sweated and lay awake cursing the mosquitoes, I slept well, having had screens put up at all the windows and nets over the beds. Citronella, garlic and rosemary also played their part in discouraging the mossies and for sheer pleasure the scents of honeysuckle and datura flowers lay on the air at night.

Chapter Seventeen

Anti-climax

There was municipal voting and Beton Ali lost his position. Another Ali came in, he was Mehmet Ali, the son of the local garage owner. I knew his father for he had been a keen fisherman and beach-dweller. All I knew about his son was that he had destroyed the quiet and peace of beach life in 1986 by installing a generator on the sand outside his *baraka* in order to run a TV set. His pleasure was to sit on his deck looking, not at the glorious panoply of the heavens, but at football and the news reports.

It speaks well for the others living near him that they complained to the authorities in Köyceğiz about the disturbing noise of the generator, with the result that we had the satisfaction one day of seeing the generator dismantled and taken away on a boat. Peace reigned once more.

I wondered whether Mehmet Ali was going to be an improvement upon Beton Ali, who lived up to, or rather down to, his name by carpeting Dalyan with concrete.

Now that the hotel complex at Iztuzu had been stopped and the Turtle Triumph evening celebrated, few of my former collaborators came to Dalyan. It was as if we had been forgotten. Aside from commercial building and a big influx of visitors, nothing happened. I was concerned about this, as I did not think we could simply rest on our laurels and turn our backs on the turtles and other wild-life.

But, as is usual with conservation matters, something new arrived to give cause for action. The SPA team themselves began building on the beach...

Of course, they had all the permissions necessary for they were the custodians of the beach. The environmentalists were not satisfied, however, and soon more experts began to arrive to see what was going on.

The buildings were to be for tourist purposes – *bufés*, toilets, changing rooms and even a first-aid post. Hundreds of bags of cement were brought to the beach and workmen began to dig foundations. I took photos and sent them to Nergis and Günther. Two geomorphologists came in response to this; they measured, examined and made reports negative to the building. They said that any permanent construction on the beach would damage the quality of the beach and cause erosion. They recommended that only wooden structures standing on stilts should be allowed. We were up against a formidable opponent though, for the builders, the SPA, were also in sole authority over the beach. Another protest from the NGOs had to do with the number of buildings, their overall mass on the beach and their sewage arrangements.

Construction continued while this mini-battle was joined. Finally it was agreed that there would be not four *restorans* but three – two at the channel end of the beach and one at Iztuzu. The changing rooms were reduced in number (indeed who could imagine the need for such in a hot climate where a minimum of clothing was worn).

An undertaking was also given that the sewage would not be dumped on the beach or in the near-by river, but pumped into tanks on a boat and removed to the Dalyan dump.

As quite often happens around here, the buildings were finished in time for the winter not the summer! To me they didn't look at all bad, with reeds on the roof and only one storey. Given the appalling lack of taste in architecture in Dalyan, these didn't shock. But I was less happy about the crazy-paving surrounds; it seemed an alien element on a beach, but we were to learn pretty soon that the new mayor had a passion for this paving and Dalyan itself was soon covered in it. Aesthetics aside, the use of stone and concrete on the sand could only prove harmful in the end. In fact, the geomorphologists have been proven correct; the beach has been eroding ever since, and the marshes; to the detriment of the reeds.

One day I found a couple of tractors laden with hefty poles, careering along by the sea's edge, throwing a pole out here and there and doing damage to nests as they went along. In reply to questions they told me their orders had come from Ankara via Muğla and these poles were to mark the demarcation line between turtles and people. I had heard about this via DHKD and AGA and didn't like the idea at all. It seemed absurd to expect a turtle to recognise this boundary and the thin end of the wedge as far as the humans were concerned. The men proceeded to hammer the poles into the sand at intervals of thirty feet ... thereby damaging more nests.

Soon the sandspit had a long line of poles running its length, ruining the harmony of the landscape and leaving thirty yards of territory for the turtles down to the sea and a hundred yards for the humans, running to the river. Also nonsense, for I myself had seen nests on the 'human' side and hatchlings' tracks near the river.

The beach umbrellas were another bone of contention with me and some turtle biologists, who said they were harmful to the nests. Nergis did not agree and accepted them. I talked to her, but to no avail. The next year, 1990, the line of umbrellas was extended and stretched for one kilometre. Each year it lengthens! Aesthetically they are also a disaster, for it was impossible to prevail upon anyone to insist upon straw ones, so the beach has earned the nickname of Coca-Cola Beach in reaction to the advertising plastered on the umbrellas.

Umbrellas are big money-spinners, however, and Dalyan municipality is said to get a hefty percentage of their rental profits.

Building had stopped at Iztuzu, of course, but the rubble and ravages left by the constructors still remained. Many biologists and environmentalists protested to Ankara, to the Council of Europe and to turtle protection groups. The thousands of tons of gravel forming a ramp on the sand was spreading with wind and tide, making the once soft sand a mess of stones, while rocks and broken chunks of cement were formidable deterrents to any turtle wanting to nest.

That year a comprehensive report about all Turkey's turtle-nesting beaches had been issued by the WWF. Their observations and recommendations were valid but no remedial action followed. Motions were tabled and reports sent around asking that the pieces be removed or ground to dust by a special machine. Promises were made, but nothing has been done about it and today the mess stretches a quarter the length of the beach.

The ramp caused more trouble, for cars and camping vans began to park there in ever-growing numbers. Obviously, the presence of campers at night was a menace to the turtles and was, in fact, illegal, but people kept coming and it was not uncommon to see a fleet of vehicles parked for one kilometre down the beach.

The warning signs which might have deterred these intruders were still not visible enough. One had to walk right up to one to read it

114

properly and there were only two such signs on the entire beach. With the winter storms they got destroyed again anyway.

No one was allowed to go to the beach at night. We conservationists had won that restriction and now I could not go myself to check on what was happening, but I heard reports of bonfires and parties on the beach at Iztuzu and of *kaptans* in Dalyan offering to take the tourists to the beach to 'see the turtles'.

It seemed to me that the conservationists needed a centre in Dalyan to co-ordinate their work and the tourists needed such to obtain information. I was constantly being approached by visitors who wanted to know about the turtles. Lily and Günther had both given me information leaflets in English and German about turtle protection in Zakynthos, but we needed something applicable to Dalyan.

A team of Turkish university students from Hacetepe University in Istanbul had been given sole permission to camp on the beach and do research on the turtles.

Riccardo, the young herpatologist from Genoa, came back to Dalyan bringing a German herpatologist with him; they stayed in my hut. Both had applied officially via their respective universities to go to the beach at night to do studies. Their permits never came, despite numerous visits to Muğla and Ankara. So they went to the beach in the daytime merely to observe tracks, but encountered problems there, for the students came and told them they would report them to the police for doing illegal studies on the beach. In September when it was too late to observe turtles and when the two young biologists were due to return home, they finally got their permits.

It was indeed sad and worrying to know that international co-operation between experts was not welcomed.

Riccardo completed his thesis on the Logger-head turtle (*Caretta caretta*) that winter and has since done important research in Madagascar. He has got his doctorate but has not been back to Dalyan. Until 1994, the students from Istanbul and Izmia Universities – the latter under Professor Baran – were doing studies on the beach.

In September I was invited to a dinner at the Greek embassy in Ankara. Lily Veneselos was guest of honour and Nergis was also invited. The theme of the evening was Co-operation on Environmental Matters Between Greece and Turkey. Ambassador and Mrs Macris, whom I knew, were our hosts.

Again it was one of those occasions, as in Athens, when I marvelled at

115

the harmonious atmosphere prevailing between these two countries who were in some conflict over Cyprus.

As far as conservation was concerned, one could only note that accord reigned.

One of the other guests present was none other than Osman Kavala, the owner of the construction firm who had been building at Iztuzu. I was introduced to him and felt a moment of panic, for he might well have had some aggressive feelings towards me ... but, in fact, he was most pleasant and told me he himself is a conservationist. In case I might have had any guilty reactions about my intervention in his Iztuzu plans, he said, 'I am glad we did not build there. The Turkish government made the right decision. We are a big company and have many other projects underway.'

Indeed Kavala Grup is one of the biggest in the country and I was positively impressed that this tycoon saw fit to be so courteous to me.

Lily looked attractive in green; Nergis her usual, beautiful self in red. I wore blue. We were photographed together sitting on a sofa – the three turtle ladies. It was a memorable and happy evening.

A few days later Lily came to Dalyan. It was her first visit and I took her to the famous beach. We walked barefoot, talking turtle, just as Nergis and I had done. Lily was more active than ever in turtle conservation and was later to found her own organisation – Medasset Mediterranean Association – to save the sea turtles.

So the year 1989 passed. I spent my first Christmas in my home. I called the house the Peaceable Kingdom, though it wasn't always that peaceful with ten cats and five dogs. No matter how many times I swore not to increase the animal population, it grew none the less. We now had a vet in the village, which was a blessing and I had had the female cats spayed. It had worked well and later the bitches were also spayed. But we always had a place for a lost, injured or needy animal.

In the village, the *belediye* (municipality) had a regular dog-poisoning programme in winter and spring. I lived in fear of my dogs falling foul of the dog-killers. My fears were alas realised when our darling Chocco, the brown son of Findik, was poisoned that winter. Metin found his body in the cotton fields near our house. Chocco had tried to get home ... we buried him in the garden and planted a tree on his grave.

I still hadn't given up hope of founding Friends of Dalyan and now it seemed more imperative than ever. We had won a certain victory with the banning of the hotel and desperately needed to consolidate by having a voice in Dalyan itself. We also had a duty – to inform the visitors about Dalyan and its flora and fauna. I had been made personally aware of this when English people, tourists in Dalyan, had come up to me saying,

'You're June aren't you? I've seen you on TV.' Many thanked me for 'saving' the turtles. I felt humbled, inadequate . . . a lot more needed to be done to save them.

Günther said he would like to form Friends of Dalyan with me. I was delighted. But it never happened. Weeks and months went by. We exchanged letters and phone calls. Then there was silence.

In May 1990, Nergis told me she and Günther were opening a Turtle Information Office in Dalyan. I was glad, though I felt a pang that my long-standing dream of Friends of Dalyan had not materialised. But, in general I was pleased for our cause and for Dalyan. We needed the prestige of an office, quite aside from its use as an educational source. They asked me to seek premises for them and I did find an empty former *restoran* on the waterfront. It needed decorating and a few essentials of furniture. Günther undertook to pay the rent, for Nergis's group was not affluent. Nergis sent some young student volunteers to man the office and I found a charming young Irishman as director. His name was John. I put him up in my hut.

Together they set about cleaning and painting and decorating the front of the building with murals depicting sea and land creatures. It was an attractive place and soon we were busy (I also helped in the office), giving out leaflets, selling posters and T-shirts and showing an excellent video film about turtles, which Nergis had made. We showed the film five to six times a day. Our visitors expressed their appreciation of the office. We received some donations and sold our modest array of stuff. We also began to collect signatures on a petition to stop shooting in the Dalyan area.

We got many signatures. People were appalled that shooting went on all over the place, despite the fact that Dalyan was an SPA – Specially Protected Area.

We also provided opinion sheets, asking for visitors' likes and dislikes. Their remarks were revealing and interesting. Our young helpers worked with zeal and pleasure. Günther sent a couple from Germany, Karin and Martin Hütter. Karin was a writer with several books on conservation to her credit. Günther had managed to get official permission for them to do a study of the beach and a count of another threatened turtle species, the Nile turtle or *Trionyx Triungius*, a soft-shelled turtle, who lives in the river near the hot springs. This dynamic couple set to work earnestly. Some of our office helpers were, however, encountering problems with locals. This was usually over girls. Some local youths would find one or more of our girls pretty, as indeed they were, but the girls would show no interest in them, as indeed, why should they? This caused friction and the usual village weapons of innuendo and gossip were used to discredit us. A shopkeeper also got nasty and 'denounced' us for selling T-shirts without a licence. It was jealousy of course and, once that shopkeeper had copied my turtle design and begun selling his pirated version, the complaints stopped. It was petty, but annoying.

The year progressed. More tourists than ever came. Tour operators in Marmaris and Fethiye were now realising what a beautiful beach we had and how desperate the tourists were for scenery, space and sand. Both Marmaris and Fethiye had become citified, commercial.

Soon the beach was getting thousands of trippers visiting daily. More boats appeared on the river. More garbage and pollution followed. At last we managed to get some bins put on the beach, but they were small and too few. In Dalyan the stench from the overflowing bins was disgusting.

The new mayor did not seem to be any more helpful to us than the last, in fact, he was negative to anyone connected with conservation and well-meaning visitors, some highly placed and knowledgeable, were chagrined to find themselves either refused a meeting with him or given short shrift in his office.

In September we closed our office. The day after, it was vandalised. Black paint was daubed over our pretty murals, all the windows were smashed and slogans like – Kill the Turtles, Out With the Greens – were scrawled on the walls.

We had signed a ten-year lease for the premises with the mayor, for the building belonged to the municipality, but when we tried to move in the following year, we found we had been manoeuvred out of the contract. The lease was given to a bank and a fortune was spent on refurbishing it. We were without an office.

For Dalyan village, however, the year ended on a high note when the Turkish daily, *Hurriyet*, carried a front-page article saying that Dalyan would receive a gift of eight and a half million Deutsch marks from the German government. The money was given as compensation for the non-building of the hotel project at Iztuzu and was said to be intended for use in installing essential services for the village, eg, electricity, water, sewerage.

These installations were certainly needed, but such an important gift could not come without strings being attached and no money arrived directly in Dalyan village. The German authorities wanted to be sure that the money would be spent in the way they wished and their ideas ran to control of the various projects. The money was to be filtered into Dalyan via the SPA team in Ankara.

On a personal level I ended the year at the Peaceable Kingdom, surrounded by dogs and cats. John, who had decided to stay the winter, helped me decorate the big salon for Christmas. We used palm fronds in place of a fir tree and made the room look pretty with tinsel and candles. The two children of my new helpers, little girls aged five and seven were invited in to get their first Christmas presents. Their faces fairly beamed when they saw our lit-up 'tree'. John and I pulled a few crackers with them – just like children too.

Chapter Eighteen

Highs and Lows

Undeterred by the desecration of our former office, Nergis and Günther joined forces again to provide a nature information office in Dalyan. I found the premises for them and they shared the cost of the rent. Both sent volunteers from Istanbul and Ankara and Germany. John was no longer in Dalyan and our office director was a nice, capable, young Turk, Gürdohar Sargul. I knew him, of course, because he had worked for DHKD for some time and often came to Dalyan or did field trips to other places for DHKD. Nergis's organisation was growing quickly, for the subject of conservation was now becoming known in Turkey. The Dalyan story promoted it. DHKD's membership was increasing and Nergis herself was a spokeswoman on environmental matters not only in Turkey, but abroad.

Günther too was very active. He continued to press for implementation of the SPA's rules relating to protection of Dalyan and to monitor the situation. His young volunteers and Nergis's were all educated, dedicated people. Usually they stayed a few weeks and were then replaced with others. We found reasonable accommodation for them locally and I invited them to my home now and again to give them a good meal. Our video was shown to many people and we got more signatures for the anti-shooting campaign.

In June Nergis organised another fund raising in Istanbul. The guest of honour was Prince Bernhard of The Netherlands. The Prince, who is a founder and patron of WWF, was guest of honour.

It was a prestigious affair attended by the British ambassador and his wife, now Sir Timothy and Lady Daunt, and a nucleus of Istanbul's elite. It was a splendid night and the dinner took place in an elegant restaurant on the shores of the Bosporous. We ate outdoors around the swimming pool.

Nergis deservedly received accolades for this successful evening. Later, we talked of old times and she told me that the WWF had decided to renew their financial support of DHKD. They had, in fact, been the original sponsors of an earlier DHKD, founded by an Englishwoman, Lady Rose Baldwin. During the course of the dinner, an award had been made to this lady for her pioneering work in conservation in Turkey.

After this event, I returned to Dalyan happy once more to rusticate in my village. I often went out on my boat to escape the hordes of trippers who were now streaming into Dalyan. Tour operators in Marmaris had hit on the idea of bringing visitors to our beach by boat from Marmaris. At first, one boat came each day, but as the other operators saw the success of their rivals, more and more boats began to arrive. The local boatmen were pleased as these trippers had to be trans-shipped to local boats in order to pass through the channel and do the river trip.

Some *restorans* were also pleased, for deals were struck and the trippers were shunted into one or other of these estaminets for lunch.

For the first time, a fee was now being charged to enter the ruins of Caunos. I knew the archaeologists working at Caunos during the summer and was particularly friendly with their leader, Professor Baki Oğun. About that time he began to complain of damage being done to parts of the site, graffiti scrawled on ancient columns and the mess left lying around by some who came there. He wanted to form a group to try to protect the area, but I, in my knowledge of the setbacks which had plagued my efforts to start Friends of Dalyan, dissuaded him.

The number of boats on the river was also increasing, as well as those coming from Ekincik with yachtsmen. Çandir, which had been a sleepy, tucked-away farming hamlet, now formed a *kooperativi* (cooperative) of boats, and turned from farming to ferrying tourists. In three years their fleet grew from 5 boats to 35 . . . many of them big and all travelling too fast on the waterways.

Once more our voices were raised, asking for implementation of the SPA rules regarding boats – these rules applied to size, length and speed – but few took any notice and boats which were too big and too fast continued to roar around the delta, making big waves and eroding the banks. Several *Triungius* turtles were found dead with injuries thought to have been caused by boats.

I went more and more to the lake, as it was less frequented. Alas! a road was being blasted in the forest around its shores. This was said to be a 'scenic' road intended to link Dalaman airport with Marmaris. Luckily, at some point, for reasons which I do not know, the work was curtailed and the road does not reach Marmaris.

At night, especially at full moon, I went to the beach and slept in my boat moored to the reeds in the river. It was glorious there in the silent night, watching shooting stars and the stately progress of the moon. In the morning, the joy of swimming in a flat-calm sea and having the beach to oneself, preparatory to a good breakfast on board. I was fully aware of my good fortune and, when the tripper boats, blaring with their Tannoy systems and rock music, began to arrive, would up anchor and return to Dalyan, there to retreat to the green oasis of my garden.

One day I saw to my dismay the old *hamam* (Turkish Bath) being bulldozed. Soon construction of an 'apartotel' began on the site – another nail in the coffin of our once lovely village. This too, had a sequel, for in time to come, the locals realised that tourists were longing to go to a traditional Turkish bath. The 'apartotel' stood empty most of the time, while other speculators set about building *hamam*s. These were modern and had little in common with the genuine article but the visitors didn't know that and *hamam*s became tourist attractions and good business.

It was known that the SPA team in Ankara were preparing a master plan for Dalyan village. When this was finally finished it showed a sprawling town of 20,000 residents, which was subsequently reduced to 15,000. Environmentalists were hard put to equate an urban project of this size with an effective nature-protection plan.

Experts continued to drift in from time to time and rumours of improvements still gave us hope. The boats were studied to evaluate their effects upon the river, flora and fauna. Nothing changed. A lady botanist from Germany did a longish field study and published her report, naming some species unique to the delta. Nothing changed. A team of entomologists did an in-depth study of mosquitoes, for these indeed were a scourge to the tourist industry. Nothing happened. The Dalyan municipality went on with its old 'remedy' which was to send a tractor pulling a tank around the village, emitting a noxious cloud of smoke (diesel and chemicals we were told) – people fled in alarm from this and those dining or drinking had to abandon their victuals as a result of contamination. None of the 'essential services' promised as a result of the German Deutsch marks materialised.

In 1991, in collaboration with Günther, a German environmentalist film-maker came to Dalyan and made another of those nature versus pollution films, including shots of the municipality sewage tanker, dumping their liquid loads near the shores of the lake.

His film, which was excellent and won an international prize, was shown in Germany and Turkey. Nothing happened in Dalyan. That is, nothing of a restraining, protective nature.

Building proliferated, though, new businesses sprang up; a second bank opened (in our former office) and a new PTT building was in operation ... all marble and intricately carved wood ... but still beset with communication problems. No one spoke any language but Turkish and frustrated foreigners waited for hours, and quite often in vain, to get through to wherever.

Construction of apartments went on apace and soon these were being sold to foreigners who found the prices attractive compared to anything in their own land. This, of course, was true. Turkey was still a cheaper place to live than the industrial countries and the big attraction was sunshine, which we had in abundance. A German speculator arrived and got permission to build a holiday village of timeshare apartments.

Package tours were now commonplace in Dalyan, whereas it had once been a place of individual travellers.

It was all a paradox. On the surface Dalyan was presumed to be a special place. Protection had been won for it and the turtles; this in turn had promoted other nature-protection projects in Turkey.

Nergis's group, DHKD, now established in new, large offices in Istanbul, was increasingly involved in projects all over Turkey: wetlands, wild flowers, bird sanctuaries, marine parks ...

I visited them about this time and was most impressed by the amount of work they were doing and the scope of that work. Nergis was also travelling a great deal, both in Turkey and abroad, in her capacity as president of DHKD an as environmental spokeswoman for her country. The membership was now above the 4,000 mark. I stayed with her and her new husband in their lovely country retreat and was able to understand better why we had seen so little of her in Dalyan in the past years. She was simply overwhelmed with work. Fortunately, her husband, Gernand, a Dutch ornithologist, proved himself to be a dynamic and competent environmentalist, thereby sharing the workload with her.

Günther, in Germany, was submerged in work too and having troubles in his own country, mostly to do with the international campaign to save endangered wild birds. Crocodiles, snakes and elephants also took his attention.

Dalyan was no longer in the limelight. Friction grew between the Germans and the Turks at our office in 1992. There was no longer the good, keen spirit there had been. Differences occurred between DHKD and AGA. In the background were the Dalyan municipality and businessmen – locals and newcomers from all over Turkey, their priorities – profit and 'development'.

In 1992, there was another fund-raising event in Istanbul. Organised by Nergis and Lady Daunt, it took place in the beautiful surroundings of the British consulate. Drinks were served in the garden, it being a fine June night and afterwards dinner in the splendid salons. Prince Philip was guest of honour. In his speech he praised the awakening interest in ecological matters in Turkey and thanked all those responsible for it. The guest list that night comprised a number of Turkish industrialists and the representatives of several international companies. Their support has been of enormous help to DHKD and to the cause of environmental protection in Turkey. A memorable night.

I went home to Dalyan and resumed my low-key lifestyle there. I put on my *kaptan*'s cap and sailed my boat – *Star of Dalyan* – to beach and lake, usually with one or two dogs decorating the prow and some friends aboard. We would take a picnic, find a quiet spot to anchor, swim, swim again and return towards evening, marvelling at the glorious scenery around us. After so many years I never tired of its beauty.

Alas! all was not well at our nature-protection office. During that summer, Günther Peter and his team were declared *persona non grata* in Dalyan. The reasons for this have never been made clear, but somehow they had trodden on some toes. I was deeply sorry. The last thing we needed was to lose helpers as loyal and useful as Günther. Without his intervention in the early years of our campaign against the hotel building, I doubt we would have won.

Our office was closed and Günther and his young helpers went to Dalaman and Patara to continue their work there. For Dalyan, although the most important nesting beach for *Caretta caretta* on this coast, is not the only one.

I was left alone: to care, to observe and to lift a restraining albeit discreet finger at any flagrant threats to Dalyan and its wildlife.

In 1993 we did not open an office. It was one of those step-backwards times. Those who suffer most are the concerned tourists, of whom there are many ... those who come to Dalyan largely because they have heard it is a place of great beauty, where nature is protected.

Many are amazed when they see the reality. Some, like me, stick around anyway, hoping, believing, it will get better. Some, like the local entrepreneurs, think it is too old-fashioned and should be exploited to its utmost.

That year ended badly – I very nearly left the village for good when four of my dogs were poisoned one night. I did not want to live any more in a place where such a monstrous thing could happen. I did not want to see my garden any more, where they used to play. I still do not know who did it nor will I ever know. It could have been a neighbour, such acts are not uncommon here; or it could have been the municipality dog-poisoners who are sent out at regular intervals with pellets of meat into which strychnine has been introduced. The hungry strays eagerly accept these titbits. I was in England at the time and it was possible my dogs strayed to the village and accepted a pellet ... but I don't think so for they all died in my garden and strychnine is a fast killer which would not have given them time to get home.

The mounds where they are buried are green now and trees grow there.

I remember them as they were, healthy and playing. So it is with the Dalyan delta. Some of it has died for me, but there is still a lot of beauty. I try to enjoy that and forget the rest.

Chapter Nineteen

Conservation Foxtrot

No matter what went on or did not go on in the village, I had always kept up my contacts with conservationists abroad and in Turkey. This presented a very different picture and was a source of hope for the future. I visited the SPA offices in Ankara on several occasions and was always reassured that legislation was being made and would eventually be enforced. Members of the organisation frequently came to Dalyan and were often in conference with the mayor. I understood that their task was not easy trying to walk the tightrope between what they knew to be good for Dalyan and its future and the local entrepreneurs' dislike of any controls that might adversely affect their plans. SPA are a fairly recently formed subdivision of the Ministry of Environment, which itself was only established in 1990. Obviously time is needed and I dare to hope that they will eventually prevail.

I was also in correspondence with NGOs and individuals in many countries. Lily Veneselos was ever more involved in protection of Loggerheads through Medasset. Each year I sent her an unofficial report of the turtles' situation in Dalyan and these were read by her at Council of Europe meetings on environment. When in London I visited the Conservation Foundation's offices. From Germany I got news from Günther.

In Istanbul and Ankara I have many good friends and it is always a delight to be with them and to know that we share similar ideas about protecting nature in their lovely country.

So the years 1994 and 1995 passed with some negative features and an increase in positive ones. Conservation is like that – one step forward, one back, quick-quick-slow, an ecological foxtrot. My old friend Professor Baki, of the Caunos archaeological team, gave me good news – Caunos is about to have a museum to display many of its

126

important finds of the past years' excavations. The Roman bath at the Caunos site will be restored and made into a museum, this thanks partly to the revenue collected from tourists.

Thanks to the tourists, too, communications at the post office have been speeded up, there are more phone lines and I now have a phone in my house.

Rubbish collection has been improved; there are clean public toilets; minibuses provide a regular summer service to Iztuzu beach. Speedboats have been banned from the waterways (alas! not respected by all); a proposed five-kilometre-long concrete 'promenade' which would have desecrated the river, has been 'postponed'. There is less poisoning of dogs, though we would like this barbaric practice to cease altogether.

On the negative side, 650 boats now ply the river and many still do not obey the rules.

Positively, night-time visits to the beach during the nesting season are banned and this rule is observed, I understand. But at least we have a coastguard officer now and I suppose he will do his duty.

In the village and its environs, building goes on unabated. The former mayor left his mark in the form of a number of statues, acres of crazy-paving and 'fountains'. Pity he didn't put the money into repairing the roads; they are full of potholes and a quagmire in winter. But we hear strong rumours that the long-promised Deutsch marks are on the way and will be used to build a sewage-disposal plant. So it goes: promises, hopes, surprises, some good.

An old friend, Daniel Farson, arrived on a visit. He hadn't been back to Dalyan for a few years, though an original beach aficionado. We took a walk around the village, he gasping in disbelief at what he now saw – he snorted at the 'fountains', dry and littered with icecream wrappers and Cola cans and cursed the crazy-paving.

'Whatever happened to Mehmet's little shop?'

'Part of a concrete shopping mall.'

'And Denizati?'

'Bulldozed and now a car park.'

'Where are the trees?'

'We've got statues instead.'

We stood in front of The Footballer, a polyester freak with head and feet too big for his body and one foot raised in the act of kicking. Dan took out his camera – 'this has to be recorded, incredible kitsch'.

'There's more,' I said, and led him under the scorching sun to The

Turtle. This masterpiece dominates the scene by the river, a larger-than-life-sized caricature of a Logger-head turtle with two monstrous-looking baby turtles nestling under its flippers ... for all the world like a mother hen with chicks would do. Dan laughed and took another snap. The polyester showed through the statue's peeling bronze paint. On the green sward where it stood, a couple of stray dogs did what dogs do on grass.

'I'll make you a wager,' said Dan. 'In ten years' time this will be the only turtle in the Dalyan area.' I shuddered. Could he be right? I did not think so, but had to admit, this was a symbol of what *Caretta caretta* stood for in Dalyan – a gimmick, a moneyspinner.

'How is the beach?' Dan asked.

'Not like in the old days,' I said, 'but not bad.'

'Let's go for a drink.' We fell into a bar, turning our backs on the river and The Turtle. Now we had the view of the tourist coaches passing by and the smell of their exhausts did nothing for the raki.

Epilogue

It is the last day of 1995 and I sit on the sand on Dalyan beach at a spot where my hut used to be. The sand has that washed look it gets in winter. The sky is blue and the sun warms me. There is not another person in sight. This is the beach as I love it best. At these times I feel once more the physical attraction this stretch of sand inspired in me the very first time I saw it from the deck of *Bouboulina*. The place touches my soul and memories stir, giving way to kaleidoscopic scenes – the turtle nesting; sunsets from the hut; the man with the knife poised to kill the turtle; the engagement party sailing under the moon; the ramshackle huts and their gypsy-style occupants; the dogs lined up at the water's edge, watching me swim; the kingfisher's colours; the hut's white curtains billowing as sails on a schooner; and I hear the sound of the sea in its different moods; I smell the wood of the hut and feel the sand under my feet – cold in morning, hot in midday.

How lucky I am to have come upon this lovely place. How privileged to have been able to make my small contribution to its well-being. How fortunate to have witnessed the activities of a shy, primeval species, its nestings, matings, to observe its shiny carapace disappear beneath the waves as it commences its long journey across the oceans.

There is a question I ask myself, one that has been raised by others in the past. Was I right to attract attention to Dalyan and the turtles in 1984? Or should I have shut up and let events take their course? Some say I accelerated the discovery of Dalyan by doing what I did. All I know is that I acted in good faith. No more could I have kept silence about the threat to the turtles, than I could have failed to intervene had I seen a child about to run into a busy road. Was I right . . . I don't know. Who does? But many visitors share my delight in this magnificent,

129

unspoiled sandspit. Most say how wonderful it is that the holiday village was not built.

In recent years we hear encouraging reports of large numbers of *Caretta caretta* nesting on Libyan beaches. No doubt this is due to the fact that mass tourism has not been encouraged there. I wonder if some of those turtles are refugees from our beach, scared off by the tread of thousands of feet that compact the soft sand in summer. It is good to know that there is a safe haven for the threatened *Caretta caretta* in the Mediterranean.

As to myself, a survivor like the turtles, I wonder where my safe haven might lie, in the event, this one is lost. As roads, buildings, power lines, discos, traffic, earth-movers, tour-operators, buzz-saws, super-markets, ostrich farms, swimming pools and urbanites encroach upon this paradise and as my own little oasis, the Peaceable Kingdom comes under siege, whither Kaptan June?

Though no longer youthful, I do not lack the spirit of adventure and discovery. Perhaps in a far corner of this planet, under a luminous sky where fair breezes blow, there is another sandspit. I like to think so and that there 'the voice of the turtle will be heard in the land.'